ALL together NOW

for aGes 4-12

13 Sunday school lessons when you have kids of all ages in one room

LOIS KEFFER
Author of ALL-IN-ONE SUNDAY SCHOOL

Group

Loveland, Colorado
group.com

Group resources really work!

This Group resource incorporates our R.E.A.L. approach to ministry. It reinforces a growing friendship with Jesus, encourages long-term learning, and results in life transformation, because it's

Relational
Learner-to-learner interaction enhances learning and builds Christian friendships.

Experiential
What learners experience through discussion and action sticks with them up to 9 times longer than what they simply hear or read.

Applicable
The aim of Christian education is to equip learners to be both hearers and doers of God's Word.

Learner-based
Learners understand and retain more when the learning process takes into consideration how they learn best.

All Together Now

Volume 2 — WINTER

Visit our website: **group.com**

Credits

Author: Lois Keffer
Editors: Christine Yount Jones, Jennifer Hooks, Lee Sparks, and Deborah Helmers
Chief Creative Officer: Joani Schultz
Cover Designer: Jeff Spencer
Interior Designer: Jean Bruns
Production Artist: Suzi Jensen
Illustrator: Matt Wood

ISBN: 978-0-7644-8231-1
Printed in the United States of America.
10 9 8 7 6   20 19 18 17

Table of Contents

The Lessons

All Together Now

Introduction

Dear Friend in Children's Ministry,

Welcome to *All Together Now, Volume 2!* In this Winter quarter, we'll make the journey to Bethlehem in Advent and Christmas, then move on to John the Baptist's introduction and Jesus' early ministry in Capernaum, and finally we'll follow the unexpected way of the King.

The journey to Bethlehem invites kids to participate in the beauty and mystery of the Advent season through the eyes of some of the key people present at that first Christmas.

God's great promise made hundreds of years before was about to come true, but in such surprising ways!

What kind of girl was Mary that God would choose her to be the mother of his only Son? What would it be like to keep God's great secret all by herself? Did being "blessed" mean taking a terrible risk that would leave her friendless and alone?

We know that Joseph was a good man, a patient carpenter. Was he all wrong about the girl he'd chosen as his betrothed? What would happen when the mighty messenger angel appeared to Joseph and made him the second person to know about God's great secret?

While the scholars of Jerusalem paid no attention, mysterious wise men from the east received God's message clearly. Most likely months before Jesus' birth, they started across the desert in hopes of finding the young king. How did these "pagans" know about God's secret, and what did their visit to Bethlehem mean?

Finally the threads of our adventures come together in a Christmas festival where Mary, Joseph, the wise men and the young Jesus joyously meet in Bethlehem!

Throughout December kids will create various Christmas crafts to take home and share with their families.

January will introduce kids to that wild man of the desert, John the Baptist. "Prepare the way for the Lord's coming!" John cries, as a quiet man from Nazareth listens at the edge of his dynamic ministry. Could it be that John's own cousin is the One he's preaching about? John doesn't even know what to tell his own disciples until he sends a query to Jesus.

Then Jesus moves about Galilee as anything but a king. With Capernaum as his home base, he works miracle after miracle and chooses disciples—including at least one very unlikely one! The miracles continue until the scribes and Pharisees don't know what to do with this young, upstart rabbi who is grabbing all the attention that should be theirs.

Obviously Jesus isn't a king in the line of Herod. He couldn't possibly be the Messiah God promised through the prophets so long ago—could he? After all, everyone knows his parents are just humble people from Nazareth. Could God be doing something special here, something so surprising that no one is ready for it?

There's only one way to find out—watch and listen with eyes and ears of faith, because there's a new adventure every week. There's only one thing you can predict about Jesus of Nazareth—he's not predictable!

Where will the way of the King lead? Walk with him and his 12 chosen friends through the dusty roads of Galilee and find out!

Lois Keffer

All Together Now

Active Learning in Combined Classes

Research shows people remember most of what they do but only a small percentage of what they hear—which means kids don't do their best learning just sitting around a table talking! They need to be involved in lively activities that help bring home the truth of the lesson. Active learning involves learning through experiences—experiences that help kids understand important principles, messages, and ideas.

Active learning is a discovery process that helps children internalize the truth as it unfolds. Kids don't sit and listen as a teacher tells them what to think and believe—they find out for themselves. Teachers also learn in the process!

Each active-learning experience in this book is followed by questions that encourage kids to share their feelings about what just happened. Further discussion questions help kids interpret their feelings and decide how this truth affects their lives. The final part of each lesson challenges kids to decide what they'll do with what they've learned—how they'll apply it to their lives during the coming week.

How do kids feel about active learning? They love it! Sunday school becomes exciting, slightly unpredictable, and more relevant and life-changing than ever before. So move the table aside, gather your props, and prepare for some unique and memorable learning experiences!

Active learning works beautifully in combined classes. Whether the group is playing a game or acting out a Bible story, kids of all ages can participate on an equal level. You don't need to worry about reading levels and writing skills. Everyone gets a chance to make important contributions to class activities and discussions.

These simple classroom tips will help you get your combined class off to a smooth start:

☐ When kids form groups, aim for an equal balance of older and younger kids in each group. Encourage the older kids to act as coaches to help younger ones get in the swing of each activity.

☐ In "pair-share," everyone works with a partner. When it's time to report to the whole group, each person tells his or her partner's response. This simple technique teaches kids to listen and to cooperate with each other.

☐ If an activity calls for reading or writing, pair young nonreaders with older kids who can lend their skills. Older kids enjoy the esteem-boost that comes with acting as a mentor, and younger kids appreciate getting special attention and broadening their skills.

☐ Don't worry too much about discussion going over the heads of younger children. They'll be stimulated by what they hear the older kids saying. You may be surprised to find some of the most insightful discussion literally coming "out of the mouths of babes."

☐ Make it a point to give everyone—not just those who are academically or athletically gifted—a chance to shine. Affirm kids for their cooperative attitudes when you see them working well together and encouraging each other.

□ Keep in mind kids may give unexpected answers. That's okay. When kids give "wrong" answers, don't correct them. Say something like: "That's interesting. Let's look at it from another viewpoint." Then ask for ideas from other kids. If you correct their answers, most kids will soon stop offering them.

How to Get Started With All Together Now

TEACHING STAFF

When you combine Sunday school classes, teachers get a break! Teachers who would normally be teaching in your 4- to 12-year-old age groups may want to take turns. Or ask teachers to sign up for the Sundays they'll be available to teach.

LESSONS

The lessons in the *All Together Now* series are grouped by quarter—fall, winter, spring, and summer—but each lesson can also stand on its own.

PREPARATION

Each week you'll need to gather the easy-to-find supplies in the You'll Need section and photocopy the reproducible handouts. Add to that a careful read of the lesson and Scripture passages, and you're ready to go!

Quick-Grab Activities—Plan in a Can

By Cynthia Crane and Sharon Stratmoen
Reprinted by permission of Children's Ministry Magazine. © Group Publishing, Inc. All rights reserved.

It's Sunday morning and you've just finished your entire lesson. You check the clock, and although the service should be ending, you hear no music, see no parents coming down the hall. What you *do* hear is your senior pastor, still excited about the message. And then you quickly begin trying to figure out what you're going to do with a room full of kids and no lesson left.

You need a survival kit. A bucket of backup, a plan in a can. So we've created two kits you can build on your own and store in your room. When you have extra time with kids, don't sweat it—just pull out your plan in a can and get busy!

In case you're wondering, Why call it a can? Why not a box or a bin or a bucket? For those times when you're worrying whether you'll be able to keep kids' attention and bust their boredom, the name is a sweet reminder that yes, you can!

PLAN IN A CAN: Games Galore!

THE INGREDIENTS

☐ Faithful Faces cards (printed photos, poster board, adhesive, and a laminator or clear adhesive vinyl) held together with a rubber band

☐ sidewalk chalk

☐ Christian music CDs for kids

☐ black-light lamp

☐ 2 large happy-face images

☐ 2 colors of plastic clothespins (enough for 3 per child; available at dollar stores)

FAITHFUL FACES ▸▸ Kids love the Memory Game, where shuffled cards are laid out facedown in a grid and kids try to find matching cards by turning over two at a time. (If they don't get a match, they turn the cards back facedown and the next person goes. If they do get a match, they get another turn.) So why not capitalize on this fun game to model and reinforce the important faithful faces in kids' lives? Just take pictures of the kids in your class, missionaries in your church, Bible friends you've been learning about, families you're praying for, and people in your congregation. Then whip up your own version of the game.

Use photo paper or regular printer paper to print out two of each photo, and mount them on poster board. Run the poster board through a laminator or apply clear adhesive vinyl, and you've got a game worth talking about. Kids will love finding their friends. And when they get a match, throw in a little challenge by giving them an extra point if they can remember names and other details about the person on the card.

SIDEWALK CHALK OF TODAY'S TALK ▸▸ Form groups of two to six, and hand out sidewalk chalk. You can have as many or as few groups as you have sidewalks for. Have groups work together to draw one picture on concrete that says something about the day's Bible story. When parents pick up their kids, you get a huge blessing: The kids tell their parents what they learned without being prompted. As a bonus, take photos of kids and their drawings for a quick recap to start off the following week's lesson. You can even make a month-in-review bulletin board starring your kids as the teachers.

MUSIC FREEZE ▸▸ If you think an hour is a long time for you, it's like dog years to kids. They have wiggles they've got to get out. So when you have extra time, turn up the music and let kids be as goofy as they want—until the music stops. Then they have to freeze in place. Give this a twist by adding a black light. Changing your environment is a great break from the everyday, and it lets kids know that you always have a few surprises in store.

CLOTHESPIN TAG ▸▸ You can use this game to remind kids that no thief can steal our joy when we go to the Joy Source: God. Place the happy-face images on the floor at opposite ends of a play area. Form two teams, and have each team go to one happy face. Assign each team a color of clothespin. Pin three clothespins to the back of each child's clothing above the waist. The goal of the game is for each team to try to steal the other team's clothespins and drop them on their own team's happy face. Play music to signal "go." Let kids play for one minute or so, and then turn off the music to signal "stop." After a few starts and stops, end the game, declare the team with the most clothespins as the winner, and then let kids get more "joy" on their backs and play again. When you're done, remind kids that they can always find new joy with God.

PLAN IN A CAN: Craft Creations

THE INGREDIENTS

- ☐ Legos in a resealable bag
- ☐ Moon Sand sculpting sand
- ☐ PlayFoam sculpting material
- ☐ window crayons
- ☐ Window Writers
- ☐ whiteboard markers
- ☐ Magic Nuudles cornstarch building blocks
- ☐ giant chenille pipe cleaners
- ☐ Bendaroos sculpting sticks
- ☐ one-subject notebook
- ☐ colored pencils
- ☐ Glitter Putty
- ☐ construction paper
- ☐ washable markers
- ☐ SuperBalls
- ☐ Christian music CDs for kids

CREATE ▸▸ If you have time to burn as kids are arriving, try this activity. Have kids use Legos building blocks, Moon Sand sculpting sand, PlayFoam sculpting material, Window Writers, or whiteboard markers to create a symbol of something that happened during the week. Then have kids show their creations as they say: "Hi, my name is _____, and I created this _____, because last week _____."

RESPOND ▸▸ Let kids use any craft supplies from the can to create a symbol of what the day's lesson meant to them. For instance, kids can draw a picture or write how they'll apply the point to life, using the windows, a whiteboard, or paper. Or they might choose to create a symbol that reminds them of what they learned, using giant chenille pipe cleaners or Bendaroos sculpting sticks. Invite kids to share what their creations represent.

PRAY ▸▸ Create a class prayer journal with a notebook for kids to write prayer notes in. Have kids all write their names on the cover because the journal belongs to all of them. Take out the journal throughout the year. Encourage kids to take turns writing their prayers or notes using colored pencils. If kids are stumped, give them prayer prompts such as "I thank God for..." "I need help with..." and "I pray for..." Close your time with prayer, and include requests from the prayer journal.

CHILL ▸▸ Give kids Glitter Putty, SuperBalls, or simply space. Play Christian music and let kids just "chill" as they quietly listen. Use the following tactile treats to help them focus on the music. As they listen, let them squish Glitter Putty between their fingers, play with SuperBalls, or simply relax on the floor at least 5 feet away from anyone else and close their eyes.

All Together Now

Mary's Story

LESSON AIM

To help kids understand that ★ *God gives us faith to do hard things.*

OBJECTIVES

Kids will

✓ play a game of trust,

✓ hear Mary tell about her encounter with Gabriel,

✓ make a Christmas ornament, and

✓ melt an ice cube in their hands as a reminder of waiting for Jesus.

BIBLE BASIS

 Luke 1:26-38

When we strip away Christmas legends, what do we actually know about the historical Mary, chosen by God to be the mother of Jesus? As we enter the four weeks of Advent, a sacred time of anticipation for Christmas, let's probe some of the traditions associated with Christmas to separate fact from fiction.

What do we know about Mary? She lived in Nazareth, a tiny village in the Galilean hills. Mary was a girl of marriageable age, probably 12 to 14 years old. It boggles the mind a bit that a young girl of that age displayed such faith and courage that God could confidently place in her womb his one and only Son.

You'll need...

☐ masking tape

☐ blindfolds

☐ copy of "Mary's Story" (pp. 16-17) printed on parchment-style paper, taped side to side and rolled like a scroll

☐ teenage actress to play Mary

☐ Bible-times costume for Mary

☐ chair

☐ scissors

☐ copies of the "Mary's Heart-of-Faith Ornament" handout (p. 19) printed on sturdy paper

☐ tacky glue

☐ 3 jingle bells per child

☐ one 18-inch and one 8-inch length of inch-wide patterned ribbon per child

☐ paper towels

☐ ice cubes (stored in a cooler so they won't melt)

☐ dish or bowl

We know very little of Mary's family circumstances. John 19:25 indicates she had a sister. But we don't know if she had brothers or other sisters, if her parents were alive at the time of Jesus' birth, if they lived comfortably, or if they were poor.

Mary became engaged to Joseph. Was Joseph an older man or close to Mary's age? We don't know. Was Mary dismayed or delighted at the proposed union? Once again, Scripture doesn't tell us.

We know a great deal about Mary's courage. She wasn't afraid to put her reputation, her family's reputation, and even her life on the line for the privilege of bearing God's Son. Becoming pregnant by another during the formal engagement period was considered adultery. Had she been charged and found guilty, one possible outcome was stoning. She chose to return to Nazareth and face shame rather than stay in the safety of her relative Elizabeth's home, some 80 miles away.

Did Mary's friends and extended family members snub her when they realized she was pregnant before her marriage to Joseph? Scripture doesn't tell us. We can assume that perhaps they did. However, it wasn't unusual for Roman soldiers or Herod's guards to kidnap and abuse young women. Some sympathetic friends might've assumed that she made up her miracle-child story to cover the trauma of such an experience.

We know that Mary found great consolation in Elizabeth's reception. It was the first time another human being confirmed the angel's message. Mary believed that the baby she carried would be the Messiah that Israel had awaited for hundreds of years.

Did the remoteness of the village and the difficulty of the times help build Mary into the young woman of purity, faith, and courage on whom God's favor rested? Had her family or families she knew suffered so under Rome's and Herod's cruel taxations that she was willing to risk everything—even her own life—to bring into the world a child who would deliver her people from such oppression?

Was she different in some way from early childhood on? more connected to God? unusually thoughtful of others? giving? a quiet loner or an exuberant extrovert? We don't know.

What we *do* know is that God chose Mary, knowing she'd be unwavering as she faced shame, fear, cultural bias, and ultimately the trauma of seeing her son die on a cross. Mary's story shows how ★ *God gives us faith to do hard things.* "For nothing is impossible with God" (Luke 1:37).

📖 **Isaiah 7:14**

In 722 B.C., Jerusalem found itself in grave danger. Israel and Syria, Judah's neighbors to the north, had joined in rebellion against the tribute demanded by the great Assyrian king, Tiglath-Pilezer III. The kingdom of Judah hadn't joined in the rebellion.

Not wanting to face possible attacks from both Assyria from the east and Judah from the south, Israel and Syria decided to strike Judah preemptively. They destroyed everything in their way, and now the city of Jerusalem was within a day's march. The citizens of Jerusalem trembled at what seemed their certain destruction.

Judah's King Ahaz wasn't a God-follower by any measure. When the prophet Isaiah advised the stubborn Ahaz to ask God for a sign, the King of Judah flatly refused. Isaiah responded,

All right then, the Lord himself will give you the sign. Look! The virgin will conceive a child! She will give birth to a son and will call him Immanuel (which means "God is with us").

King Ahaz of Judah couldn't have imagined how far-reaching Isaiah's prophecy would be. He did see, however, that in answer to Isaiah's prayers, Tiglath-Pilezer's armies showed up to pour retribution on Israel and Syria before they could take another step toward beleaguered Jerusalem.

It's wonderful to serve a God so great that his answers to our prayers go way beyond anything we could ask or imagine.

UNDERSTANDING YOUR KIDS

Can you think of a 12- to 14–year-old girl who might come close to the qualifications God required of Mary? Given the difference in our cultures, that question might elicit a chuckle or two.

Today's young women often don't consider marriage until they're approximately twice that age. Our life expectancy is far longer and infant mortality rates considerably lower. Girls now can get an education equal to that offered boys, something unthinkable during biblical times. Even after marriage, couples today often elect to wait until they've gotten advanced degrees and purchased a home before getting into the business of childbearing.

So Mary's story, when explained in accurate historical context, may be somewhat shocking to your kids. It's great to have this information in your pocket to explain how our culture is very different from Mary's.

THE LESSON »

ATTENTION GRABBER

Rescue!

Greet kids warmly and welcome them to your first Advent lesson.

Say: **Advent is a four-week time when we wait for the fulfillment of God's promise that he would send a Messiah, a Savior for the whole world. It's a time of trusting and hoping that God will keep his promise.**

Just about everywhere in the Bible we see that God doesn't do things the way people expect. That first Christmas was no exception. God surprised everybody involved and worked in a way that demanded their absolute trust.

It's easy to *talk* about trusting God, but when it comes to *doing* it in an everyday situation, well, it can be harder than you think. I'll show you exactly what I mean.

Have everyone line up on the masking-tape line. If you have seven kids or fewer, ask for an older willing child to be a Rescuer. If you have eight or more kids, ask for two Rescuers. Have the Rescuers stand with their backs to a wall and facing the other kids.

Distribute blindfolds to the children standing on the masking tape line.

Say: **Those of you on the line will be the Walkers. I'll explain what that means in just a minute. Help each other get your blindfolds on nice and tight. Taller kids, kneel down so smaller kids can help you. When you're all blindfolded so you can't see, I'll explain how our game works.**

Check the kids' blindfolds to make sure they're secure but not too tight. Then line up the blindfolded players on the masking tape line again and give the following instructions: **When I call your name, start walking toward the wall. Walk at a normal pace—not timidly as if you're afraid you're going to hit something. Your Rescuer will catch you before you hit the wall, turn you back toward the line, and give you a light push in the right direction. Again, walk at a normal pace back toward the line.**

When you reach the line, I'll stop you and turn you back toward the wall. You'll walk at a normal pace again, depending on your Rescuer to stop you before you hit the wall. When I clap my hands, it means someone is close to the wall—so slow down.

Prep Box

Before class, make a masking-tape line on the floor approximately halfway across the room.

All Together Now

Call on a young child to repeat the rules of the game before you begin.

At first, pace the game slowly by allowing a couple of seconds of lag time between calling children's names to start walking. The game will naturally move more quickly once everyone's walking. Shout, "Go, go, go!" for kids to pick up the pace even more. Keep an eye on your Rescuer(s) to help them; clap your hands before anyone walks into the wall.

If you have time, play another round so Rescuers get to be Walkers.

Ask:

- **What was hardest thing about playing this game?**
- **Describe how you felt when I sped up the game.**
- **Why did—or didn't—you have faith in your Rescuer?**

Say: **Today we're going to meet someone very famous from the Bible. This person knew that if she obeyed God, there'd be difficult consequences. It'd be like walking straight into a wall. She had to trust God to be her rescuer in a big way. She showed how ★ *God gives us faith to do hard things.***

It was this person's choice to make: She had to choose whether to obey God or step back and say, "No thanks— better find someone else for this job."

This person? A young girl from Nazareth named Mary. Here's something to keep in mind: When these events took place, Mary was probably somewhere between 12 and 14 years old.

Here's her story.

BIBLE EXPLORATION
....

Mary's Story (Luke 1:26-38)

Go to the door to welcome your teenage Mary. Turn to the children.

Say: **Look at this! Mary herself is visiting us today!**

Escort Mary to the sitting area you've created for her. Then sit and join the kids as a listener.

Prep Box

Beforehand, recruit a young teenager to play the role of Mary. Give her the script a week ahead of time so she'll have plenty of time to practice. Arrange for her to have a simple Bible-times costume with a long head-covering. Set up a simple sitting area for her in your room. Ask her to linger in the hallway of your room just before your Bible story.

Mary's Story

My name is Mary. I'm just an ordinary girl from a tiny village called Nazareth. Have you ever heard of it? Probably not. It's in Galilee, a small province, part of the vast Roman Empire. The Roman soldiers and our own evil King Herod control everything we do. Taxes are heavy. Herod takes more than his share to pay for building his grand palaces. The Romans tax us to the edge of starvation.

If people can't pay, the soldiers may take their land or whip them harshly. When we hear the horses we run and hide, but if they want to find us, they will.

(Bow your head to pray.)

O Lord God of Israel, please deliver us from those who would crush the life out of the good people of this village! Let us serve you in freedom!

This morning I was a maiden, free to run and play with the other girls of my age. Now I'm to be Joseph's wife! I must veil my face in public and behave like a married woman, even though I won't enter Joseph's house for a year!

(Bow your head to pray.)

O Lord, is this truly your will for me? If it is, will you give me an obedient heart, because I feel anything but obedient right now!

(Stand and take a few steps from the chair.)

You'll never believe what happened to me this evening! At first I thought I was daydreaming when an angel called my name. But then I looked up and saw the light. My daydreaming quickly turned to terror!

"Don't be afraid," the angel reassured me. Then he went on to tell me terrible and wonderful things. God was pleased with me and soon I would have a child, the Son of God. His name would be Jesus, and he would reign over Israel on King David's throne forever!

(Sit down again.)

I didn't understand how these things could happen, but the angel said, "Nothing is impossible with God."

But what will my family think? What will Joseph think? Will he still want me for his wife? Will anyone want me for a wife?

I answered, "I am the Lord's servant. I will do whatever God wants."

(Bow your head to pray.)

O Lord, if what the angel said is true, this child could be the Savior we've all been praying for! This little Jesus could change things for my people—forever! This is from you. You will be my rescuer and my strength.

(Rise and leave the room quietly.)

After Mary has left the room, form a circle.

Ask:

• **Now that you've heard Mary's story, what do you think about her?**

• **When have you had to face something that was really hard?**

• **How did Mary show trust in God?**

Say: **Mary knew that accepting God's invitation to be Jesus' mother meant that she'd face many challenges. But she also knew that she could trust God to get her through those challenges—he'd protect and rescue her each step of the way. Mary was a great example to show us that ★ *God gives us faith to do hard things.***

LIFE APPLICATION

Mary's Heart-of-Faith Ornament

Lead kids to your craft area where you've set out your supplies.

Say: **Mary could only take this difficult assignment from God because her heart was full of faith in God. This Christmas craft will remind you of Mary's life just as it's written about in the Bible.**

Help kids tie a bow with the shorter ribbon at the top of the long ribbon. Then have them slide three jingle bells onto the long end of the ribbon and tie the ribbon and the bells into a loose loop at the very end. Finally, have kids cut out the three hearts and space them down the center of the ribbon. Have them use tacky glue to hold the hearts in place.

As kids work, encourage them to tell you where they'll hang their ornaments or if they'll give them away.

Prep Box

Set out copies of the "Mary's Heart-of-Faith Ornament" handout, scissors, tacky glue, jingle bells, and an 18-inch length and an 8-inch length of inch-wide patterned ribbon for each child. Also make a sample of the Mary's Heart-of-Faith Ornament beforehand to give kids an idea of what they'll be making.

All Together Now

Mary's Heart-of-Faith Ornament

Mary must have had strong faith in God to accept the job of being Jesus' mother. Let's celebrate her story with a beautiful Christmas ornament!

1. Tie a bow at the top of the ribbon.

2. Tie a loop with three jingle bells at the bottom of your ribbon.

3. Cut out the three hearts. Space them nicely down the ribbon and glue them in place.

God sent the angel Gabriel to Nazareth, a village in Galilee, to a virgin named Mary. She was engaged to be married to a man named Joseph, a descendant of King David. Gabriel appeared to her and said, "Greetings, favored woman! The Lord is with you!"

Luke 1:26-28

Mary asked the angel, "But how can this happen?"... The angel replied..."Nothing is impossible with God."

Luke 1:34-37

Mary responded, "I am the Lord's servant. May everything you have said about me come true."

Luke 1:38

COMMITMENT

. . . .

Waiting

Distribute paper towels, and say: **In just a moment I'm going to let you choose an ice cube. I don't want the melting ice cube to freeze your fingers, so fold your paper towels to provide some protection for your hands.**

Have kids form a circle, and pass around a dish of ice cubes. Say: **Cover your ice cube with both hands to make it melt more quickly.**

Ask:

• How long do you think it'll take for us to melt our ice cubes?

Let several kids share their opinions.

Say: **Israel waited more than 700 years from the time of Isaiah's prophecies until Jesus was actually born.**

That was about 10 lifetimes if you go by today's standards, but many more in Bible times. During that time the city of Jerusalem was attacked and destroyed. God's Temple was destroyed and all its treasures carried away. Many of Israel's people were taken to the far-off land of Babylon, never to return to their homeland.

Ask:

• Tell about the longest time you've ever waited for something to happen.

• Describe how it feels right now to wait for your ice cube to melt.

Say: **Only God knew the perfect time to send Jesus into the world. Only God could see that Mary of Nazareth was the one to be Jesus' mother. Only God knew about the events he'd already set in motion and the people he'd already chosen to surround baby Jesus at his birth. Yes, it was a long time, but it was also God's perfect time.**

The wonderful thing is that God's people never stopped believing. They kept hoping in God's promise of Jesus, year after year, century after century, even when the waiting was sometimes uncomfortable, messy, and painful—just like holding this ice and waiting for it to melt is a little painful.

This month of Advent we remember that time Israel spent hoping and waiting—hundreds of years compared with our one month!

Collect kids' ice cubes and paper towels in a trash can.

All Together Now

CLOSING

A Prayer of Waiting

Say: **Let's close with prayer.**

God, it can be hard for us to wait for Christmas, even for a few weeks! This season of Advent, help us remember the faithful people who for hundreds and hundreds of years kept believing in your promise of a Messiah. We can't imagine a world without Jesus. Thank you, God, for sending him to us at just the right time. If we can trust you to do that, we know we can trust you with all the small things that come into our lives every day.

Prepare our hearts for this wonderful season. In the name of your Son, Jesus Christ, we pray, amen.

Joseph's Story

Lesson 2

LESSON AIM

To help kids realize that ★ *God leads us in surprising ways.*

OBJECTIVES

Kids will

✓ play a game that involves getting their directions mixed up,

✓ hear the Bible story from Joseph,

✓ create a Christmas triptych, and

✓ express their trust in God, no matter what direction he takes them.

BIBLE BASIS

read

 Matthew 1:18-24

As with many people in the Bible, we wish we knew more of the "facts" about Joseph, who served as Jesus' earthly father. Here's what we do know: he was from Nazareth, a carpenter by trade, of David's ancestry, and engaged to Mary. When he saw that Mary was pregnant and the child was not his, Joseph's first thought was to divorce her quietly. Then an angel appeared to him in a dream and assured him the child was from God, so Joseph took Mary as his wife.

You'll need...

☐ blindfold

☐ copies of the "Christmas Triptych" (p. 31) printed on sturdy white paper

☐ copy of the "Joseph Trusts God" story (pp. 28-29) printed on parchment-style paper, taped side to side and rolled like a scroll

☐ scissors

☐ markers

☐ 3 paper plates (or pieces of paper): a smiley plate, a straight-faced plate, and a frowny plate

☐ Sticky Tack adhesive (available at office supply stores)

☐ optional: glitter glue

Matthew gives us an important clue about Joseph's character:

Joseph, her fiancé, was a good man and did not want to disgrace her publicly, so he decided to break the engagement quietly (Matthew 1:19).

It makes sense that God would want his Son to be raised by a good man.

Joseph, like Mary and Zechariah, received a visit from an angel as part of the account of the birth of Jesus. Unlike Mary's and Zechariah's dramatic visitations from Gabriel in Luke, Joseph is visited by unnamed angels in his dreams to lead him quietly through his fears and difficult choices. (Matthew 1:20; 2:19-20; and 2:22). A visit from such heavenly beings undoubtedly marks someone as holding a very special place in God's plan.

Having decided to quietly leave Mary after learning she was pregnant with a child not his, an angel visits Joseph in a dream and lets him in on the heavenly secret about Jesus. Joseph awakens and follows the angel's instructions to take Mary as his wife and to raise Jesus as his own. Joseph then follows God's leading (via angels) to protect his family from the murderous family of Herod. Don't you wonder about the conversations that might've played out between Joseph and Mary as the baby grew? Why was God keeping this secret from everyone else? How different would the little Jesus be? When would *he* know God's plan? Would they be adequate parents at all? Why did God choose them?

 **Isaiah 9:6-7**

These famous verses from Isaiah reflect hundreds of years of hope for the Messiah. George Frederic Handel set the verses to his famous chorus "For Unto Us a Child Is Born" in "Messiah." In 587 B.C., Nebuchadnezzar's armies destroyed Jerusalem, pulled down the city wall, and burned the Temple and carried its treasures off to Babylon. Seventy years later, a delegation of Jews returned to rebuild the city wall. Then another delegation came to rebuild the Temple. Hampered by the Samaritans, it was a stop-start operation. Over the years, the Temple was desecrated, cleansed, and rededicated. When Herod the Great came to power shortly before Jesus' birth, he disassembled that Temple and built an even greater one. The Jews were a captive people who longed to remain faithful to their unique relationship with God. They believed that the Messiah would free them from the bonds of captivity and with

All Together Now

a mighty sweep of his hand banish the powers who had for so long taxed and terrorized their small nation.

The people in Herod's family, whom Rome had appointed to rule Israel, were in a word, loathsome. Their hunger for power led to executions within their own family. They had no scruples about digging too deeply into the pockets of their fellow Jews for taxes whenever a royal project called for it.

Yes, the Jews longed for the child who was to be born, the son who was to be given. But they weren't ready to accept the humble Messiah God had in mind, born into the family of an earthly father who was no more than a carpenter from a lowly village such as Nazareth.

Once again God says, "Surprise!"

UNDERSTANDING YOUR KIDS

You'll most likely have children who have a "go with the flow" attitude and others who get upset if the routine falls apart. This isn't a measure of faith—it's a difference in personality. If, as a parent, you've ever raised one of each, you know what a challenge it can be!

Use this lesson to encourage your kids to trust in God and feel secure in his plans, even as those plans change before their eyes.

THE LESSON »

ATTENTION GRABBER

All Turned Around

Greet kids and have them form a circle.

Say: **Now I need a brave child to stand in the center of our circle.**

Blindfold the child, and then say: **Spin around several times until you're feeling a little dizzy. OK, now take a few spins in the other direction. Excellent. Next, walk toward the outside of the circle with both your hands outstretched to guide your way. When you touch someone, stop. Everyone else, stay totally silent.**

Have the kids forming the circle clasp hands so your wanderer doesn't wander away.

Say to the blindfolded person: **When you've found someone, gently touch the person's hair, shoulders, nose, cheeks, and chin, and then drop your hands.** Pause a few moments for the blindfolded person to accomplish this.

Say: **Tell us who you think is in front of you.**

If you have seven or fewer kids, give each child just one guess. Whether the guess is correct or not, give the child a round of applause for courage.

Give other children a chance to be in the center. The game moves quickly enough that everyone should be able to play. Take a turn yourself if there's time. To keep it challenging, have kids in the circle scramble while the child is spinning.

After everyone has played, retrieve the blindfold and form a circle again.

Ask:

- **What was fun about this game?**
- **What was difficult about it?**
- **When have you felt that your life was as unpredictable as this game?**

Be prepared to share with kids a time in your life when God led you in a different way than you planned.

Say: **When we live our lives hand in hand with God, life is never dull.** ★ *God leads us in surprising ways.* **We make our plans, but many times God has different ones, better ones, that he slips in. We may not know what to think of the changes in our lives when they happen, but when we keep trusting God over the long run, we always see that he**

All Together Now

had something in mind that was too grand for us to even understand at first.

    We're going to learn from someone who put a lot of trust in God. He lived in Nazareth and owned a carpentry shop. The Bible doesn't give us many more details than that.

BIBLE EXPLORATION

Joseph's Story (Matthew 1:18-24)

Say: **I need help with sound effects for our Bible story.**
Form three groups. Assign these sound effects to each group:

GROUP 1
Something mushy to say when they hear the name *Mary.*

GROUP 2
Carpenter sound effects like hammers and saws when they hear the word *woodshop.*

GROUP 3
Walking sound effects when they hear some form of the words *walk over.*

Joseph Trusts God

Joseph had his eye on her for some time. Oh, yes. Mary *(pause)* was a lovely girl. Joseph could always see Mary *(pause)* walking over *(pause)* to be kind to someone, to give a smile, to lighten a sad heart.

Joseph was in his woodshop *(pause)* when he told his brother that he was going to walk over *(pause)* and speak to her father about a marriage price for Mary *(pause)*. Joseph's brother said, "Joseph, why would you want a young girl like Mary?" *(Pause.)*

Joseph ignored him and just kept working in his woodshop *(pause)*.

His brother scowled and walked over *(pause)* to his own house.

Joseph got the go-ahead from her dad to marry Mary *(pause)*. But when Joseph walked over *(pause)* to tell Mary *(pause)*, she wasn't happy. Bummer! Joseph headed back to his woodshop *(pause)*, thinking, *Given a little time, she'll come around. I'm sure of it.*

The next day, Joseph left his woodshop *(pause)* and walked over *(pause)* to Mary's *(pause)* house. She wasn't there. She had walked over *(pause)* on a journey to her relative Elizabeth's house. Joseph wondered if they had a woodshop *(pause)*.

When Mary *(pause)* came back, she broke Joseph's heart. Nothing in his woodshop *(pause)* could fix it. Joseph walked over *(pause)* to her and could see that Mary *(pause)* was going to have a baby.

Joseph wanted to walk over *(pause)* to her father and tell him that he would divorce Mary *(pause)* quietly. But Joseph had a dream in his woodshop *(pause)* that night that changed everything.

In his dream, an angel's voice shook the room as he said, "Joseph, son of David, do not be afraid to walk over *(pause)* and take Mary *(pause)* as your wife. For the child within her was conceived by the Holy Spirit. And Mary *(pause)* will have a son, and you're to name him Jesus, for he will save his people from their sins."

That morning Joseph barely staggered out of bed. *Who am I that the angel of the Lord should visit me?* he wondered. *And what kind of task has he put before me—that I should help raise the Son of God?*

Joseph walked over *(pause)* to Mary's *(pause)* house. He said, "O Mary *(pause)*, my sweet Mary *(pause)*, I've thought wrong of you! Together we'll keep the secret that God has given us: that the child growing in you is from God himself! I will care for you, Mary *(pause)*, and for you, little Jesus. Oh, yes! I will be the best father I can!"

After you've returned to your original appearance, ask:

• Joseph experienced a big surprise. Tell about a time you had a big surprise.

Say: **Poor Joseph must've felt terrible to discover that Mary was going to have a baby. In Bible times, an engagement was the same as a marriage. In the eyes of the law, they were married. So Joseph didn't have any easy choices about what to do with Mary. He couldn't just call off the engagement. He'd actually have to divorce her.**

One visit from an angel changed everything in Joseph's life (snap your fingers) **just like that. It's true that ★ *God leads us in surprising ways.***

Ask:

• **Why do you think God chose a humble carpenter and a young girl to be Jesus' parents on earth rather than making Jesus a regal king with servants and riches?**

• **What's surprising to you about the way God chose Jesus' earthly parents?**

LIFE APPLICATION

A Christmas Triptych

Today we're going to create a triptych—a work of art in three pieces. In the early days of Christianity, triptychs were sometimes used as art for altars, or ceremonial tables.

Our triptych will tell a little bit about Joseph and little bits about us. Today we learned from Joseph's life that ★ *God leads us in surprising ways.*

Let's take a look at our triptychs and see how we'll express that.

Demonstrate how kids will cut out the triptych so that when the sides are folded in, it becomes a closed window.

On the left side, have kids draw about a time God led Joseph in a surprising way. On the right side, challenge kids to draw about a time God led them in a surprising way. Kids may also wish to decorate the illustration of Bethlehem with markers and glitter glue.

Have kids each sign their creations and encourage them to talk with their parents about surprising ways God has guided their families as they show them their triptych at home. They may also wish to ask their parents to set up their triptychs behind a glass-contained votive candle.

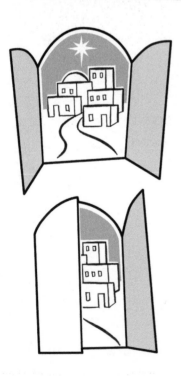

Prep Box

Set out copies of the "Christmas Triptych" handout, scissors, and markers.

All Together Now

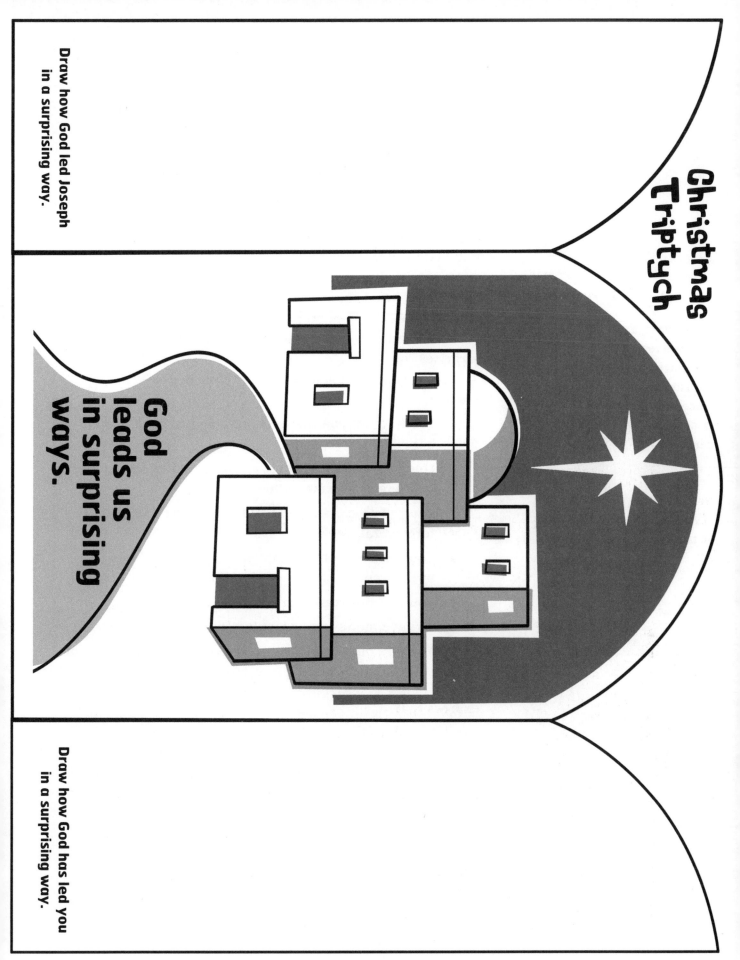

Draw how God led Joseph in a surprising way.

God leads us in surprising ways.

Draw how God has led you in a surprising way.

Published in *All Together Now, Volume 2* by Group Publishing, Inc., 1515 Cascade Ave., Loveland, CO 80538.

31

COMMITMENT

. . . .

Life's Surprises

Say: **We know about the big surprises God planted in Mary's and Joseph's lives. Let's find out how you might react to surprising news in your life.**

Gather kids in the center of the room. **If the surprising change I read would be hard for you, run to the frowny face. If it'd be easy for you, run to the smiley face. If it wouldn't make much difference, stay by the plate with the straight face. Ready? Let's go!**

After each "surprise," ask:

• **How can God make something good happen out of this surprise?**

• **How could God help make this change easier to accept?**

✓ **You find out your parents are going to have another baby.**

✓ **One of your parents gets a job in a different city and you're going to move there.**

✓ **You're in a car accident and have to be in a big cast for several weeks.**

✓ **Your parents tell you that you can't have the big birthday present you've been hoping for this year.**

✓ **You find out your best friend is moving far away.**

✓ **To save money, your family gets rid of the television.**

✓ **You find out your parents are getting a divorce or that your parent is getting married.**

After finishing the game, say: **No matter what we plan for in our lives, things happen that we don't expect or even want. Joseph certainly didn't expect what happened with Mary and Jesus. But he followed God anyway. If we're open to following God no matter what, ★ God leads us in surprising ways.**

CLOSING

....

A Prayer for Faith

Form a circle.

Dear God, we know that life doesn't always go the way we expect it to. God, during those times, will you give us extra, hang-on-tight faith? Because we know that in the end, you have a beautiful plan in mind. In Jesus' name, amen.

The Mysteries of the Wise Men

LESSON AIM

To help kids realize that ★ *those who seek God will find him.*

OBJECTIVES

Kids will

✓ play a finding game,

✓ create signs or symbols to tell the story of the wise men,

✓ make a starlight candle craft, and

✓ commit to seeking God in new ways.

BIBLE BASIS

 Matthew 2:1-12

The wise men (also known as the Magi) are the most puzzling group of people to enter the Christmas scene. It's almost amusing to see how they took the ever-paranoid Herod by surprise. What? A claimant to his throne who'd come from outside his scheming family? From an unpretentious little village like Bethlehem? Scholars assume from the name *Magi* that the wise men were from Persia, where they could've been exposed not only to the old prophecies of Daniel, but also to the Jewish communities who'd never returned from the exile. While their primary work may have been as astronomers and astrologers, they were also known as interpreters of dreams.

You'll need...

☐ thimble or other small object

☐ 3 Bibles

☐ poster board in different colors

☐ markers

☐ scissors

☐ copies of the "Starlight Candle Ring" handout (p. 41) printed on sturdy paper

☐ votive candle

According to historical accounts, they had a hand in determining the choice of a king. They were highly respected seekers of wisdom.

Judging from the value of the gifts they brought and their ability to undertake a months-long trip to Bethlehem, they must've had great wealth at their disposal and likely dressed appropriately to their station.

The Bible never says how many wise men there were. The tradition of three is based on the number of gifts presented to Jesus: gold, frankincense, and myrrh. There could've been two, four, five, or many more. But three fits well with one of our favorite Christmas carols, "We Three Kings."

The important thing about their visit was their affirmation to a young mother and her husband that God had shared the secret of this young Messiah with seekers of the truth in a faraway nation. And for the first time, Herod had an inkling that a different sort of challenge might arise to test his rule.

📖 Zechariah 8:22

In the well-known passage from Matthew, the wise men fulfill the less well-known ancient prophecy of Zechariah 8:22: "Many peoples and powerful nations will come to Jerusalem to seek the Lord of Heaven's Armies and to ask for his blessing."

For hundreds of years the Jews thought that the coming Messiah was for them *alone*. They trusted that the Messiah would rise up as a national hero who'd unshackle them from the bonds of conquering nations. It's ironic that non-Jewish wise men were more in tune with God's plan than the Sadducees, Pharisees, or teachers of the law.

But before we point fingers, let's take a long look in the mirror. I've survived enough of God's "big surprises" that I don't go into a special "woe is me" room to wail and gnash my teeth anymore. But as far as catching the beauty in God's big picture, I'm still in class 101.

The more time I invest in seeking God for his own sake, the more open I become to great possibilities appearing out of nowhere and the less I fret about my plans.

Follow the example of the wise men. Consider the night sky and the greatness of God. Rest in that greatness. Consider that our great God calls you beloved. Let God's love and grace minister to you. Who knows? Like the wise men, you may receive joyful news of God's nearness, for ★ *those who seek God will find him.*

UNDERSTANDING YOUR KIDS

Kids love the mysterious "kings" who appear in the Christmas story. Men of wealth, men of mystery. Wow! Kids would love to receive visitors like that any night. And a special star—how cool is that? This is a true story that's better than Saturday morning cartoons.

But I wonder...if kids were constantly seeking God with the diligence of the wise men, how much more often would they be delighted with the wonders God shows them every day?

Encourage your kids to be constant seekers of God. Because ★ *those who seek God will find him.*

THE LESSON »

Find the Thimble

Greet kids as they arrive. Encourage them to tell you about their family plans for Christmas. When everyone is ready, say:

To begin today, we're going to play a simple game. But here's your challenge: Just because our game is simple doesn't mean it's easily solved.

Show your thimble.

Say: **While your faces are hidden, I'm going to hide this thimble somewhere in the room. When I say, "Find the thimble," you'll begin looking. When you think you've found it, call out, "I spy!" Don't touch the thimble, just point to it. Then we'll all come to see whether you really found it.**

We'll play several times. Don't be surprised if the thimble is harder to find than you think!

Have kids hide their faces against a wall of the room. The object is to keep the thimble in fairly plain sight. Here are some suggested places to hide it:

- ✓ on a finger
- ✓ under a room divider
- ✓ under a chair
- ✓ on a piano key
- ✓ on top of a room divider
- ✓ on the shelf of a whiteboard
- ✓ on the floor against a wall

After several searches, form a circle.

Say: **Even as we played round after round of this game, you kept right on searching for the thimble. You didn't get distracted and you didn't get bored. Your goal was to find the thimble and you kept at it.**

We're going to work together to tell today's Bible story. We're going to learn about men who were searching for the Messiah God promised. They looked for clues about the Messiah. When the men decided they had enough evidence to prove that the Messiah had been born, they organized a caravan and started across the desert on a months-long trek full of danger at every turn. Nothing would stop them from finding the Messiah God promised!

BIBLE EXPLORATION

Here's Your Sign (Matthew 2:1-12)

Form three groups, making sure to mix readers and nonreaders, and set out Bibles, scissors, markers and the different colors of poster board. Groups will work together to create props to tell the Bible story.

Assign the following verses to each group:

GROUP 1:
Matthew 2:1-4

GROUP 2:
Matthew 2:5-8

GROUP 3:
Matthew 2:9-12

Tell groups that for each verse in their Scripture passage, they need to create a sign or symbol that'll help tell that part of the Bible story. For example, they could make a yellow star for verse 2.

Allow time, and then call kids back together.

Read the verses chronologically, allowing groups to each display their signs or symbols to help tell the story.

When the story has been read, have groups lay out their signs and symbols. Then form a circle around the symbols. Have kids each give a gift of affirmation to the child on their right by selecting a sign or symbol for that child. For example, children might say, "I chose the star for you because you shine with God's love all the time." Or they might say, "I chose the gift for you because you are a gift from God to me." It's OK if signs or symbols are repeated.

Ask:

• **How easy or difficult was it to find ways to give each other the gift of affirmation?**

• **How easy or difficult is it to find ways to seek God?**

• **What are some ways we can seek God this week?**

Say: **Sometimes all we have to do to seek God is to stop and look around. The way a leaf twirls to the ground will remind us that God made this amazing world. A friend's smile will remind us that everyone is created in God's image. Looking at the night sky shows us how limitless and powerful God is.**

Like the wise men, we can be seekers of God. We'll talk more about that in just a minute. Right now, let's make some candle rings to help us remember that ★ *those who seek God will find him.*

LIFE APPLICATION

Starlight Candle Ring

Lead your kids to your craft area.

Say: **A mysterious star beckoned the wise men to cross the desert in search of a baby boy they believed would be the Savior of the world. Let's make this beautiful starlight candle ring to remind us that** ★ *those who seek God will find him.*

It's best to demonstrate this craft step by step and have kids follow along. Say: **We'll work with partners, with older kids helping younger kids.**

- ✓ Cut out the large rectangle containing both halves of the candle ring.
- ✓ Fold the candle ring in half horizontally; then cut out the four diamonds.
- ✓ Cut the two halves of the candle ring apart. (The diamonds you just cut will now become open triangles.)
- ✓ Fold crisply on the dotted lines and cut out the four stars. Cut outside the lines, so no remaining marks show on your candle ring.
- ✓ Cut the slits at the end of both halves of the candle ring.
- ✓ Turn the halves so the slits fit together. Make sure to connect the slits on the inside, so the outside of the candle ring looks smooth.
- ✓ Pinch the corners with the cut-out stars so the candle ring becomes a square.
- ✓ Remind kids to ask for a parent's help to find a suitable glass-enclosed candle to place in the middle of the candle ring.

Teacher Tip

Before class, set out copies of the "Starlight Candle Ring" handout and scissors. Also have a sample of the candle ring displayed with an appropriately sized votive candle so kids can see a sample of what they'll make.

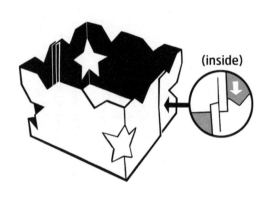

(inside)

All Together Now

Starlight
Candle Ring

In search of the Savior, the wise men followed an unusual star across the desert to the town of Bethlehem. Make this festive starlight candle ring to remember that those who seek God will find him. Use your candle ring with a parent's help around a glass-enclosed votive candle.

COMMITMENT

. . . .

Seeking God

Holding the thimble from the opening game, gather kids in a circle on the floor.

Say: **Learning to seek God can make a bigger difference in your life than you can imagine. And you can start at any age! Let me explain it like this: It's kind of like playing Hide-and-Seek, only you** *want* **to be found—by God. So learn to just stop a minute and take a deep breath, because God is the one who does the finding!**

It's simple, really. It's letting your heart be quiet and making space for God to speak to you. It might be saying a favorite Bible verse and then just being quiet afterward. It might be setting aside a special place in your room that you keep for being with God. It might be going on a walk and being quiet the whole way so God can talk to your heart. Right now, just be quiet with God.

Here's how our little game will work. I'm going to tell one way I'll seek God this week. Then I'll toss the thimble to my friend [name] across the circle and [name] will tell one way [he/ she] will seek God this week. Then [name] will toss the thimble to another person and so on.

After we share a way we'll seek God this week, we'll move back out of the circle and the circle will close the space where we were. That way only the people who haven't played yet will be in the circle as it grows smaller and smaller. Got that? Let's begin!

Continue tossing the thimble and making the circle smaller until all the children have expressed one way they'll seek God this week.

CLOSING

. . . .

Prayer for God-Seekers

Have the children hold hands and follow you in line. Turn the line as you walk until the children end up forming a tight spiral around you.

Pray: **Lord, thank you for your promise that those who seek you with all their hearts will surely find you. Remind us, Lord, to take time to seek you this week, just as the wise men came so far to seek you. We have faith that you'll find us in special moments and connect our hearts to yours. In Jesus' name, amen.**

All Together Now

Christ Is Born!

LESSON AIM

To rejoice that ★ *God sent his Son, Jesus, to save the world.*

OBJECTIVES

Kids will

✓ decorate the room for a Christmas festival,

✓ make Christmas candle treats,

✓ travel to a "cave" in a hillside above Bethlehem to hear the Christmas story, and

✓ create an Advent calendar to take home.

BIBLE BASIS

 Luke 2:1-20; Matthew 2:9-11

It's a great idea to read this beloved passage of God's Word before you prepare for this lesson. Don't hurry through it. Grab a mug of warm cider, sit in a comfortable armchair, and ask God to take you back to the village of Bethlehem when it was bursting at the seams with travelers thanks to the order of Roman emperor Caesar Augustus.

So our Messiah, King of kings and Lord of lords, is born in a stable among gentle beasts because the world is going about the business of paying taxes. God didn't send a deposit to the innkeeper saying, "Please reserve your best room for my son. He'll be arriving tonight."

You'll need...

☐ Christmas carol music

☐ basket of unbreakable Christmas decorations

☐ Sticky Tack adhesive, paper clips, and stick pins in a sealed plastic bag

☐ kitchen timer

☐ cake doughnuts,* pretzel sticks,* and gumdrops* in a paper grocery bag

☐ napkins

☐ electric candles

☐ small Nativity set

☐ adult male to play a Roman tax collector

☐ copy of the "Tax Collector's Script" handout (p. 50)

☐ copies of the "Advent Calendar" and "Advent Calendar Numbers" handouts (pp. 52-53) printed on sturdy white paper

☐ kid-friendly Bibles

☐ paper and pens or pencils

☐ scissors

☐ tape

☐ optional: Roman uniform

☐ optional: glitter glue

* Always check for allergies before serving snacks.

Thank you, Jesus, for being born among the least of us. At some point in our lives, we'll each learn what it means to be *one of the least of these*. It could be any of a hundred things that sends us there—the loss of a job and identity, a foreclosure, the death of a beloved one, a catastrophic illness or accident. When we suddenly find ourselves in that category, it's a wondrous thing to find ourselves in the arms of a Savior who was born and died in that category himself.

No, the Jews didn't see their Messiah arrive as a knight on a white charger to drive out the Romans. Instead, to Bethlehem that night there came a Savior who lives among us, knows our suffering and sorrow, takes the worst that death offers, and rises triumphantly. The Son of God came quietly into a broken world. He still comes quietly to meet us in the broken places of our lives.

Hallelujah! You're most welcome here, little Lord Jesus.

 **Micah 5:2**

The little village of Bethlehem first gained major notice in the Bible as being King David's birthplace and the place of his anointing as future king of Israel. The prophet Micah referred to Jesus when he stated that a future ruler would come from Bethlehem. Once again, Jesus fulfilled prophecy as the "one whose origins are from the distant past."

A ruler like King David was exactly who the Jewish people were longing for—unstoppable on the battlefield, charismatic, a devoted follower of God who would make the name of God respected among the nations. And after all, God had promised to keep David's line on the throne of Israel forever (2 Samuel 7:16). Joseph, the earthly father of Jesus, was descended from David's royal line. And the Roman census had put Joseph and Mary in the right place during Jesus' birth. Still, no one was quite ready for Jesus, king of the universe, to be born king of our *hearts*.

UNDERSTANDING YOUR KIDS

For some kids and their families, the month of December is so packed with programs, concerts, and other obligations that the arrival of Christmas Day is actually a relief from stress. This is such a contrast to the purpose of Advent and Christmas. Advent is a time of both restraint and anticipation, a time of honoring the hundreds of years God's people waited between the messianic prophecies in the Old Testament and their fulfillment.

All Together Now

The proliferation of lights, obnoxious mall ornaments, in-your-face sales, and grating music in stores bears little resemblance to the reality of a small, conquered nation waiting, waiting, waiting for salvation.

Think of what strides you've made in helping kids understand that Christmas is ever so much more than the day when we get stuff. It's the day when the longings of nations are fulfilled in a far deeper way than anyone could ever anticipate.

Enjoy leading kids through today's Christmas festival, including its surprising trip to a cave above Bethlehem. The impressions you leave with kids today will stay with them forever.

ATTENTION GRABBER

Christmas Festival!

As kids arrive, have joyful Christmas carols playing. Point to a basket of unbreakable Christmas decorations including red and green ornaments, glittering garlands, ornaments, artificial Christmas flowers, and any other items you have on hand. Include Sticky Tack adhesive, paper clips, and a few stick pins in a sealed plastic bag.

Say: **Welcome to our Christmas festival! The long wait of Advent is finally over. Today we celebrate Jesus' birth!**

Let's begin by speed-decorating our room. First, form groups of three. Help kids get in groups if you need to. **Good. In just a moment I'm going to toss this basket of decorations all over the floor. With your group, take a couple of decorations and see how quickly you can decorate one area of our room. This isn't a contest—we're all just having fun. Once I let you have the decorations, I'll set a timer for five minutes. When the timer goes off, we're done decorating!**

Stand back, because here come the decorations! Whoosh!

Toss the decorations so they'll spread out across the floor. Decorate with the kids, offering suggestions if necessary, until the timer goes off.

Hey—look around at this fabulous room! It's beginning to look a lot like Christmas! Now scoop the unused decorations back into the basket and I'll tell you what I've got planned next. Lead kids to a table where you've placed the bag with the cake doughnuts, pretzel sticks, and gumdrops.

Every festival needs decorations and every festival needs treats. I ask for your full attention as I perform the amazing feat of turning these three simple items (remove the doughnuts, pretzel sticks, and gumdrops from the bag) **into a Christmas candle.**

Place a doughnut on a napkin. Push a pretzel stick into it so the doughnut becomes the candle holder. Push a bright-colored gumdrop on top of the pretzel stick to serve as the flame. Shape the top of the gumdrop to a tip. Hold up your candle.

Say: **Did you see how simple that was? In just a moment you can make your own edible candles. But you can't eat them right away. You can eat them before we're done, just not right away. So just don't get too hungry too fast, OK?**

Teacher Tip

If the pretzel sticks are too long and heavy for the doughnut to hold them securely, you may want to break them off to an appropriate height.

All Together Now

Have the kids line up to pick up their ingredients one by one: first a napkin and a doughnut, then a pretzel stick, and then a gumdrop.

Say: **Once everyone has a candle, we'll make our trip to Bethlehem. Let's get going!**

BIBLE EXPLORATION

The Road to Bethlehem (Luke 2:1-20; Matthew 2:9-11)

Have kids line up behind you at the door to your room, candles in hand. Remind them that you'll need to take a quiet journey in order to not disturb other activities that are going on in the building.

As you lead everyone out the door, say: **These last few miles to Bethlehem are rocky and steep. A cold breeze has picked up because the sun has dipped beneath the horizon. If we stay in a tight group, we'll be warmer. Be ready to catch anyone who trips over a rocky place. If we just stick together and take our time, we should be fine on this narrow trail.**

As you lead the kids, pretend to find your footsteps very carefully on the "rocky" path. Stop every now and then to continue the story.

Say: **We'll arrive in the little town so late, I'm not sure we'll find anyone awake. You know, back in Bible times, people pretty much went to bed when the sun went down. They didn't have candles like the ones we're carrying. They had small lamps that burned oil. But oil was expensive, so most people got up when the sun rose and didn't stay up too long after it set.**

Continue carefully on your journey. Point out large rocks here and there that kids should avoid. Save the next bit of dialogue until you're close to your Bethlehem. It'll be the signal for your Tax Collector to jump out and confront you.

I don't think they'll have closed the city gates, because people coming for the census and to pay their taxes are swarming the city at all hours. We'll have to be careful not to disturb anyone, though.

Tax Collector appears suddenly and blocks the road.

Tax Collector: **Thought you'd sneak around and not have to pay your taxes, did you?**

Prep Box

Beforehand, lay out a winding path through your church that'll land you in a small, fairly dark room, such as a utility or storage room. You'll need enough space for you and the children to gather for the story, but no more. You might use a corner of a choir loft or a landing on the way to a balcony. Poke around your church for a creative spot that you'd never thought of before as a teaching spot.

In the space, leave a few electric candles and a small, simple Nativity set.

Finally, arrange for someone posing as a Roman tax collector (costume nice but not necessary) to jump out and challenge you just before you reach your Bethlehem destination. This will provide a great moment of drama for the kids! The script for the Tax Collector is on page 50. Provide a copy of the script to your Tax Collector a week ahead of time so he or she can become familiar with it.

Teacher: **Why, uh, no, sir. We're just strangers trying to find our way to Bethlehem.**

Tax Collector: **Well, you've found it, haven't you? Now, what family are you from?**

Teacher: **Well, I'm from the** [use your own name] **family. But each of these children is from a different family.**

Tax Collector: *(puzzled)* **I never heard of the** [name] **family. Are you sure your hometown is Bethlehem?**

Teacher: **Uh, my hometown is** [name where you live].

Tax Collector: [repeat the town]**?** *(rubbing chin)* **Are you sure that's in Judah?**

Teacher: **With all due respect, sir, it's in** [your country's name].

Tax Collector: **So you're not Roman citizens?**

Teacher: **I hope not, sir. We're tourists, you might say.**

Tax Collector: **I'm not sure we have any taxes for tourists.**

Teacher: **I'm glad to hear that, because we didn't bring any money. We just came to worship the Christ child.**

Tax Collector: *(moving past the teacher and addressing the children)* **Who is this Christ child? Speak up. If you can tell me I'll let you pass.**

When several children have answered, Tax Collector nods his head and signals the kids to pass, and then walks down the road and disappears.

Say: **Whew—that was a scary moment! I was proud of the way you explained to the tax collector who the Christ child is! You stood right up to him. Good for you!**

Look—our destination is just ahead. Let's hurry!

Lead the children into the room you prepared beforehand. Have them gather in a story circle. If there's a door, close it.

Say: **We've just had quite an adventure. Now I'd like you to help me create a quiet, worshipful atmosphere. Here we are at the cave where baby Jesus was born. Are you surprised I said cave when the Bible says stable? There wasn't much wood to spare in the hills around Bethlehem. And there were lots of open caves in the hillsides. You can still see them today! It's likely that Joseph took Mary to a cave where they would have been sheltered on three sides. And there would've been extra body-warmth from the animals—maybe oxen or donkeys—that were probably around.**

All Together Now

You know, if I'd been Mary, I might have wondered, *Lord, won't you provide a place for your Son to be born?* But God *did* provide a place, the lowliest place imaginable. Jesus Christ, the Son of God, came to earth and was born among animals in a stable.

Say: **God keeps on doing things in surprising ways, doesn't he? The problem is that the Christmas story is told so often that it's easy to miss some of the surprises God offers.**

Form groups of three and give each trio a kid-friendly Bible. Within each group, have a willing child read Luke 2:1-20 and Matthew 2:9-11 while the other two write or draw what surprising things they hear in each Bible passage. After about five minutes, bring all the groups together.

Ask:

• **What surprises did you find in the Bible passages?**

• **Why do you think God would choose for Jesus to be born in a stable?**

• **Why do you think God doesn't tell us in advance exactly what he's going to do and why, rather than surprising us?**

Say: **After being part of this great adventure, you must be hungry. Go ahead and enjoy your snacks as we discuss the story.**

Ask:

• **If you could be one person in the Christmas story, who would it be? Why would you choose that person?**

• **What do you think the shepherds might have told others when they left the stable?**

• **What do you suppose the wise men might have said to Joseph and Mary?**

• **What's important about God sending all these special visitors to the stable that night?**

• **If you had a chance to bow before baby Jesus, what would you say?**

Say: **Our visit to Bethlehem is almost over. Let's pray together.**

Ask kids to join you in a silent prayer, or let a willing child say a prayer thanking God for the gift of his Son.

Let's hurry right back to our Christmas festival. We still have lots of fun things to do!

Tax Collector's Script

Dear Volunteer Tax Collector,

    Thank you for volunteering for a few minutes to provide some startling drama for our Sunday school kids on their way to Bethlehem. The teacher will discuss with you the right place to jump out and confront this group of foreign travelers, demanding that they pay their taxes. The teacher will engage in a short dialogue with you, and then your service to our Sunday school kids will be done. The shock you give them may stay with them a while, though—we love to make the Word of God memorable!

Appear suddenly and block the road.

TAX COLLECTOR: Thought you'd sneak around and not have to pay your taxes, did you?

TEACHER: Why, uh, no, sir. We're just strangers trying to find our way to Bethlehem.

TAX COLLECTOR: Well, you've found it, haven't you? Now, what family are you from?

TEACHER: Well, I'm from the [use your own name] **family. But each of these children is from a different family.**

TAX COLLECTOR: *(puzzled)* **I never heard of the** [name] **family. Are you sure your hometown is Bethlehem?**

TEACHER: Uh, my hometown is [name where you live].

TAX COLLECTOR: [repeat the town]**?** *(rubbing chin)* **Are you sure that's in Judah?**

TEACHER: With all due respect, sir, it's in [say your country's name].

TAX COLLECTOR: So you're not Roman citizens?

TEACHER: I hope not, sir. We're tourists, you might say.

TAX COLLECTOR: I'm not sure we have any taxes for tourists.

TEACHER: I'm glad to hear that, because we didn't bring any money. We just came to worship the Christ child.

TAX COLLECTOR: *(moving past the teacher and addressing the children)* **Who is this Christ child? Speak up. If you can tell me I'll let you pass.**

When several children have answered, nod your head and signal the kids to pass, and then walk down the road and disappear.

LIFE APPLICATION

Advent Calendar

Say: **Today we're going to make a craft that you can use every year to remember the amazing Christmas stories we've learned about together.**

Distribute the handouts.

You're going to cut out the numbered squares and tape them in order to the Advent calendar. Start with number 1 at the bottom left of the tree, and count until you have number 10 placed at the top. Put them precisely in place so the Bible verses are covered. Let's form pairs, older kids with younger ones, to make sure the squares are in the right place before you tape them on one edge only.

Have kids work together to tape their calendars and then sign their calendars on the back. You may also want to have kids decorate the calendars with light touches of glitter glue.

Starting 10 days before Christmas, you can begin to read through these Bible verses, one each day. Begin with number 1. The verses will remind you of how God brought everything together just right to ★ *send his Son, Jesus, to save the world.*

Prep Box

Beforehand, lay out copies of the "Advent Calendar Numbers" and "Advent Calendar" handouts, scissors, tape, and glitter glue on a workspace. Create a sample calendar for kids to follow.

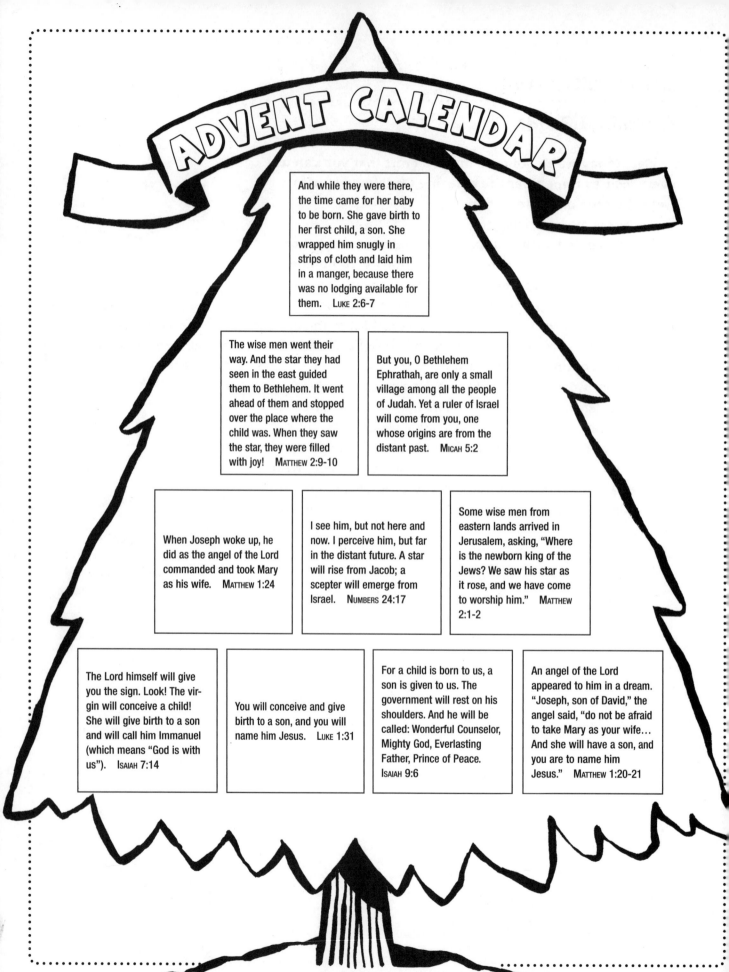

ADVENT CALENDAR

And while they were there, the time came for her baby to be born. She gave birth to her first child, a son. She wrapped him snugly in strips of cloth and laid him in a manger, because there was no lodging available for them. LUKE 2:6-7

The wise men went their way. And the star they had seen in the east guided them to Bethlehem. It went ahead of them and stopped over the place where the child was. When they saw the star, they were filled with joy! MATTHEW 2:9-10

But you, O Bethlehem Ephrathah, are only a small village among all the people of Judah. Yet a ruler of Israel will come from you, one whose origins are from the distant past. MICAH 5:2

When Joseph woke up, he did as the angel of the Lord commanded and took Mary as his wife. MATTHEW 1:24

I see him, but not here and now. I perceive him, but far in the distant future. A star will rise from Jacob; a scepter will emerge from Israel. NUMBERS 24:17

Some wise men from eastern lands arrived in Jerusalem, asking, "Where is the newborn king of the Jews? We saw his star as it rose, and we have come to worship him." MATTHEW 2:1-2

The Lord himself will give you the sign. Look! The virgin will conceive a child! She will give birth to a son and will call him Immanuel (which means "God is with us"). ISAIAH 7:14

You will conceive and give birth to a son, and you will name him Jesus. LUKE 1:31

For a child is born to us, a son is given to us. The government will rest on his shoulders. And he will be called: Wonderful Counselor, Mighty God, Everlasting Father, Prince of Peace. ISAIAH 9:6

An angel of the Lord appeared to him in a dream. "Joseph, son of David," the angel said, "do not be afraid to take Mary as your wife… And she will have a son, and you are to name him Jesus." MATTHEW 1:20-21

Published in *All Together Now, Volume 2* by Group Publishing, Inc., 1515 Cascade Ave., Loveland, CO 80538.

ADVENT CALENDAR NUMBERS

Published in *All Together Now, Volume 2* by Group Publishing, Inc., 1515 Cascade Ave., Loveland, CO 80538.

53

COMMITMENT

Circle of Christmas

Invite kids to bring their calendars and join you in a circle.

Say: **Christians have been using Advent calendars for hundreds of years to help them prepare for Christmas. The calendars helped them learn to be patient as they prepared for the coming of the Savior. Many families use their Advent calendars in the evening just before bedtime as a family devotion—you could do that with your family at home, too. Let's look at our calendars right now.**

Ask a willing child to read the verse behind window #1 and explain how it's important to the Christmas story.

Say: **The next night you'll open window #2 and do the same thing.**

Ask a second child volunteer to read the verse behind window #2 and explain its importance to the Christmas story.

Say: **You'll keep going every night like this, and then you'll open the last window on Christmas morning. Now here's how you'll use it this year. Today is December [ ]. There are [ ] days until December 25. That means you'll read [ ] verses every night so you'll have one last verse to read on Christmas morning. Some families like to open the last window on Christmas Eve.**

Ask:

• **Why do we open just one window a day, rather than the whole thing all at once?**

• **What are some ways people get ready for Christmas?**

• **How could reading the Bible help prepare us for Christmas?**

Say: **Now, write your name and age on the back of your calendar. This is a good reminder of when you created your calendar, because you'll be able to enjoy these Advent calendars for many, many years.**

Make sure kids all leave with their calendars at the end of class.

CLOSING

....

Closing the Festival

Say: **Wow! We've had a very busy Christmas festival morning. Let's pray.**

Dear God, even though we celebrate Christmas every year, it always seems brand new to celebrate the birth of your Son, Jesus. We're so glad ★ *you sent your Son, Jesus, to save the world.* **In Jesus' name, amen.**

Let's close today by singing the famous Christmas carol "Away in a Manger."

The Mysterious Prophet

LESSON AIM

To help kids grow in their ability to ★ *tell others about Jesus.*

OBJECTIVES

Kids will

✓ be challenged to taste a mystery treat,

✓ find clues about John the Baptist and discover what the Gospels say about him,

✓ make a necklace of John's Life Savers candies, and

✓ practice using their John's Life Savers candy necklaces to tell others about Jesus.

BIBLE BASIS

📖 **Matthew 3:1-17; Mark 1:1-11; Luke 1:5-25, 39-45, 57-66, 3:1-22; John 1:19-34**

John the Baptist remains one of the most mysterious and compelling figures in the entire Bible. Luke 1 tells about his birth: He was born to Elizabeth and husband Zechariah, a priest. Elizabeth was Mary's relative. Zechariah first heard the news of Elizabeth's pregnancy from the angel Gabriel when it was the old priest's turn to serve in the Temple at Jerusalem. His reaction to Gabriel? "How can I be sure this will happen? I'm an old man now, and my wife is also well along in years" (Luke 1:18).

You'll need...

☐ chocolate-covered raisins* in a covered dish

☐ honey*

☐ wet wipes

☐ copy of the "The Mystery Man" handout (p. 62)

☐ kid-friendly Bibles, such as *The Hands-On Bible®*

☐ scissors

☐ transparent tape

☐ whiteboard

☐ paper

☐ pens or pencils

☐ 18 inches of yarn per child

☐ 4 Life Savers candies* per child

☐ copies of the "John's Life Savers" handout (p. 65)

☐ glue sticks

* Always check for allergies before serving snacks.

Because he was slow to believe, the angel rendered Zechariah silent and unable to speak until the baby was born.

Mary went to visit Elizabeth and Zechariah while she was pregnant with Jesus (Luke 1). Little John leaped in Elizabeth's womb when Mary came near.

After this in-the-womb encounter, the Bible doesn't record any contact between Jesus and John until John emerges from the desert as a "wild man" prophet who's actively engaged in his ministry before Jesus begins his own.

What happened to John in the intervening years? Here lies the mystery. Due to his parents' advanced ages, he may have been a young orphan. By Jewish custom he would have likely followed his father into the priesthood. If he became a priest, why did he leave the priesthood? We don't know. At what point did he take off for the wilderness and begin living like a wild man? The fact is he lived like many of the Old Testament prophets, especially Elijah. He provided a dynamic, living link between the Old Testament and the New Testament.

John knew his mission: to prepare the way for someone greater who was about to appear, to ★ *tell others about Jesus.* He lived in the wilderness, honed and chiseled by the Spirit until he was ready to take on the arena of unfaith and immorality that Israel had become. Then he roared out of the desert like a mighty wind, the first prophetic voice in 400 years. His charisma was so great, his message so compelling, that people came in droves to hear him preach and to be baptized. The Roman governors and their Jewish rulers were always afraid of an uprising among the Jews. John the Baptist gave them plenty of reason to worry. When he dared to publicly criticize the immorality of Herod Antipas, ruler of Judea, Herod had John thrown in jail. John would later be martyred for his unwavering faith and convictions.

John remained true to his one solitary mission: to prepare the way for Jesus. When Jesus came to John for baptism, the latter found himself in a conundrum. How did it make sense to baptize the one he'd been preparing the people to receive? But the blessing in the end was John's, for he was allowed to see and hear the heavenly affirmation of Jesus as God's Son, in whom God was well pleased.

 Isaiah 40:3-5

Matthew 3:3 clearly states that the Old Testament prophet Isaiah was speaking about John in these words: "He is a voice shouting

All Together Now

in the wilderness, 'Prepare the way for the Lord's coming! Clear the road for him!' " In Old Testament times, it was customary for a traveling monarch to send messengers ahead to smooth any obstacles in his way and to assure a fitting royal reception. In many ways, John provided this service for Jesus.

When the angel announced John's birth to Zechariah, the angel said, "He will be filled with the Holy Spirit, even before his birth. And he will turn many Israelites to the Lord their God. He will be a man with the spirit and power of Elijah. He will prepare the people for the coming of the Lord. He will turn the hearts of the fathers to their children, and he will cause those who are rebellious to accept the wisdom of the godly" (Luke 1:15-17).

UNDERSTANDING YOUR KIDS

Kids will be intrigued by the "rough 'n' ready" John the Baptist. They probably don't know anyone like him. They might compare him to "mountain men" characters they've seen in movies and on TV.

People who want to be heard today rent out huge venues and charge enormous ticket prices so audiences can have a glimpse. In John's case, crowds tramped miles into the countryside to hear this compelling prophet tell them to clean up their lives and turn their hearts back toward God.

You can explain that there's one great difference between John the Baptist and today's great audience getters: Our mysterious prophet was filled with God's Spirit, on a mission from God to ★ *tell others about Jesus,* and privileged to introduce the one and only Son of God!

THE LESSON »

Mystery Treats

Greet kids and have them form a circle. Show them the covered dish containing the chocolate-covered raisins.

Say: **I hope one of your New Year's resolutions is to be brave, because I have some absolutely delicious treats in here, but I'm not going to tell you what they are. I will just tell you that they are** *sooo* **delicious that some people can hardly stop eating them once they start. They're** *that* **good. I promise. Besides, tasting our mystery treats will give us a couple of important clues about the mystery man in today's Bible story.**

So, everyone, close your eyes. Nice and tight—that's right. Not even a tiny bit of peeking. If you're ready to try my super-duper delicious treat, cup your hands in front of you and I'll drop a few in your hands. No peeking while you chew and swallow.

I'll tell you this: You'll be disappointed if you don't try these! But try them or not, no peeking at all! And, once you've had a taste, no talking, either.

Distribute your chocolate-coated treats to kids who have their hands cupped.

Pause as kids eat their mystery snacks.

Say: **OK, you can open your eyes now, but don't say anything about what you ate. I hope you enjoyed your mystery treat.**

Good news: I have another treat for you! Same deal as before. This time I want you to hold one hand out flat, like this. Demonstrate holding your hand out flat, palm up.

Say: **This time, while you keep your eyes squeezed shut, I'll come around and place a drop of this mystery treat onto the palm of your hand and you can lick it off. I promise you, you won't regret it! This is mmm-mmm good. Here we go. Hold out your palm if you're brave enough to give it a try.**

Go around the circle squeezing a bit of honey on each child's palm. As kids lick it off, say: **Remember, not a word about what you're tasting. Let's keep it a mystery!**

OK, open your eyes but keep your lips sealed. I'll pass around wet wipes and you can clean that sticky substance off your hand. Let kids clean their hands with wet wipes.

Ask:

• **Describe the second treat you just tasted.**

Say: **The first mystery treat is a little harder though, and I'm going to see if I can fool you with it.**

Ask:

• **If the first mystery treat was fried locusts— grasshoppers—dipped in chocolate, how would you feel?** Let kids be grossed out and offer their thoughts.

Say: **I hope you didn't believe me, because that wasn't the treat! Not even close! It was just chocolate-dipped raisins!**

The idea of eating locusts grosses out many people. But the truth is that for a lot of people who lived in the desert back in Bible times, locusts were a staple food. Honest! Locusts are full of protein and fat, and unlike other foods, they're usually abundantly available in the desert.

Ask:

• **Tell how easy or difficult it was to trust me with the food I gave you to eat.**

• **Now tell how easy or difficult it is to trust what others say about God.**

Say: **You've just learned important clues about our mystery Bible prophet: He lived in the desert and ate locusts and wild honey.**

Today we're going to learn a lot about how to ★ *tell others about Jesus.* **We'll focus on the person who was a mysterious prophet, but also whose entire life was devoted to telling others about Jesus—before Jesus even began his ministry on earth.**

BIBLE EXPLORATION

The Mystery Man (Matthew 3:1-17; Mark 1:1-11; Luke 1:5-25, 39-45, 57-66; 3:1-22; John 1:19-34)

Say: **I've planted several clues about our Mystery Man around the room. There are 12 clues all together. Make sure you don't look for a second clue until everyone has found at least one clue. Once we find all the clues, let's gather around the whiteboard. Are you ready? Start hunting!**

As kids find the clues, tape them to a whiteboard or wall.

Prep Box

Before class, copy the "Mystery Man" clues (p. 62) and cut them apart on the solid lines, fold them in half on the dashed lines, and tape them in various hiding places around the room.

The Mystery Man

was related to Jesus	ate locusts and wild honey
lived in the desert	wore a tunic made of camel's hair and a leather belt
acted like an Old Testament prophet	told people to turn away from their sins and live pure lives
told people that someone was coming who was far greater	told people that the kingdom of heaven was near
huge crowds of people came out to hear him	baptized people in the Jordan river
baptized Jesus and heard God's blessing on him	his preaching made the teachers of the law angry

Published in *All Together Now, Volume 2* by Group Publishing, Inc., 1515 Cascade Ave., Loveland, CO 80538.

Say: **Hmm—today's person from the Bible sounds like a really interesting guy, doesn't he? Some of you may have studied about him before, so if you already know who he is, keep it to yourself for now.**

Ask:

• **Tell which clue about our Bible mystery man is the most interesting to you.**

Say: **Let's find out about our Bible mystery man for ourselves.**

Form four smaller groups. (A "group" can be one child, as long as he or she can read the Bible.) Pass out Bibles, paper, and pens or pencils. Assign each small group one of the four Gospel accounts of John the Baptist (see page 61) to read and report on. (For Luke, use 3:1-22.)

Say: **Working as a team, find and read the portion of the Bible I've assigned to your group. Find out the name of the mystery man. Then list five things you think are strange about him and five important things he did. Pick a person who'll report back to the entire group about what you learn about our mystery man. You'll have about seven minutes.**

Before time is up, give a one-minute warning. Gather the group back together when time is up. Ask each group to report on what they learned. It's okay if there are repetitions, such as "John lived in the wilderness."

Ask:

• **What's the most interesting thing you learned today about John the Baptist?**

• **Why was John fearless when telling others about Jesus?**

• **What things can make us afraid to tell others about Jesus today?**

Say: **People crowded to the Jordan River to hear this strange person preach about turning away from their sins. Unlike most people, John wasn't concerned with trying to make a big name for himself. Quite the opposite—he knew Jesus was coming very soon. John wanted to make a great name for Jesus. John knew he was there to prepare the way by telling everyone he could about Jesus. God wants us, in a similar way, to ★ *tell others about Jesus*. Let's look at a fun way to do that today.**

....

John's Life Savers Necklaces

Prep Box

Before class, set out copies of the "John's Life Savers" handout, scissors, glue sticks, Life Savers hard candies, and 18-inch lengths of yarn for each child.

Lead kids to the craft table where you've set out the supplies.

Have kids cut out the three paper Life Savers. As they cut, talk about the fact that these were John the Baptist's three main messages when he preached: turn away from sinning, turn toward God, and get ready for the Savior.

Show kids how to lay out their necklaces in the following order: a hard candy, a paper life saver, a hard candy, a paper life saver, a hard candy, a paper life saver, and a hard candy. Have kids fold the paper over the yarn and glue the sides together. Help kids tie a knot at the beginning and end of the decorative part of their necklaces to keep the decorations front and center.

Have kids help each other tie on their necklaces.

COMMITMENT
....

Necklace Bearers

After kids have cleaned up their craft area, form a circle for discussion.

Ask:

• **What can we learn from John the Baptist about** ★ *telling others about Jesus?*

• **How can you carry on John's work today?**

• **How can your necklace help you** ★ *tell others about Jesus?*

Ask for willing pairs of kids to role-play how they might use their necklaces to tell others about Jesus.

CLOSING
....

John, Our Example

Ask:

• **What's one thing you admire about John the Baptist?**

Say: **John surely knew he'd face opposition from the king and the religious leaders, but he wasn't about to let that keep him from sharing the message God gave him.**

All Together Now

John's Life Savers

Sometimes we're a little shy about telling people about God. Whenever we feel shy, remember John the Baptist. He looked like an awesome, powerful man of the desert, and he acted the same way. He had a message from God and nothing was going to keep him from telling it. Let's ask God to give us that same readiness and courage.

Dear God, thank you for letting us learn about someone who bravely told about Jesus. When we have a chance to tell someone how wonderful Jesus is, we pray that you'll give us all the power and courage you gave John. In Jesus' name, amen.

Jesus Is Here!

LESSON AIM

To help kids see that ★ *Jesus' teachings and healings are amazing.*

OBJECTIVES

Kids will

✓ experience excitement over a dream come true,

✓ dress up friends as sick people and have "Jesus" heal them,

✓ create a pop-up craft to help them share faith at home, and

✓ reflect on wonderful things Jesus is doing in their lives.

BIBLE BASIS

📖 Luke 4:31-44; 5:12-16

After John baptized him, Jesus went into the wilderness for 40 days to be tempted by Satan. Having passed that test, he returned to his home area of Galilee to begin his ministry. And what a ministry it was!

Desiring to keep the fact that he was God's Son a secret, Jesus commanded even the evil spirits he cast out to keep from speaking his name. Perhaps this was so he could walk freely among the townspeople, teaching and healing.

Galilee was a rustic, unsophisticated area. Everything that was fine, educated, and sophisticated came out of Jerusalem

You'll need...

- ☐ blank envelopes and paper
- ☐ pencils
- ☐ a large box
- ☐ box of shawls, strips of cloth, blankets, and washable markers
- ☐ Bible-times costume for your Jesus actor
- ☐ copy of the "Capernaum Skit" (p. 73)
- ☐ leper's statement ("Lord, if you are willing, you can make me clean.") printed on an index card
- ☐ copies of the "Jesus Is Here Pop-Up" handout (p. 75)
- ☐ scissors
- ☐ transparent tape
- ☐ thin ribbon
- ☐ craft knife
- ☐ hole punch
- ☐ optional: room decorations, such as potted palms, clay jars, foam rocks, striped blankets
- ☐ optional: markers, glitter glue

and its surroundings. In Galilee, Jesus could carry on a mostly unopposed ministry of God's love. So he set up his home base in the seaside town of Capernaum. He taught there every Sabbath day, and "people were amazed at his teaching, for he spoke with authority" (Luke 4:32). In this area, he called his first disciples. There he healed Peter's mother-in-law, the Roman officer's servant, and the man lowered through the roof. Astonished by these miracles, people gathered and brought their sick to wherever they thought Jesus was likely to appear.

What a tender picture of God Jesus shows us here. Imagine the gasp when Jesus *touched* the man with leprosy. What an act of love for one who'd been untouchable for so long.

In Galilee we see Jesus reaching out to the hearts of a hopeful people, teaching them that God is not only holy and to be feared, but also loving and tender, longing to bring healing and hope to hearts who have so long hungered for him.

📖 Isaiah 61:1-2

When Jesus emerged from the wilderness after 40 days, he returned to his home area of Galilee, where his fame quickly spread as he regularly taught in the synagogues "and was praised by everyone" (Luke 4:15). That was, with one huge exception: the synagogue in his hometown of Nazareth. At Nazareth, he went to the synagogue, where he was handed the scroll of the Scriptures, unrolled the scroll and found Isaiah 61:1-2. After reading it, Jesus announced, "The Scripture you've just heard has been fulfilled this very day!" (Luke 4:21)...Wow! That would quiet a busy synagogue. Jews would immediately understand his statement to mean, "This prophecy is talking about me, and now—here I am!"

The people in Nazareth were "amazed by the gracious words that came from his lips" (Luke 4:22). However, they couldn't accept Jesus, the hometown boy whose family they knew, as the Messiah God had promised. The crowd was ready to push him off a cliff, but Jesus walked right through the crowd, left his hometown, and went to Capernaum instead. It's likely he never came back to his hometown after being rejected by it.

UNDERSTANDING YOUR KIDS

Today, some of the loudest voices at schools and in politics teach that there's something good to be drawn from every religion

All Together Now

and that Christians are narrow-minded for declaring that Jesus is the only way to God.

A few days following Jesus around the towns of Galilee would make a surprising difference for those who classify Jesus as "just another teacher." Here he handed out grace upon grace, teaching people about a side of God they'd never known before, healing the suffering and welcoming people of all classes—both those the Jews considered clean and those they considered unclean.

What a model to challenge our kids to follow on their faith journeys!

THE LESSON »

ATTENTION GRABBER

Scattered Dreams

As kids arrive, recruit one of your older kids to act the part of Jesus during the Bible story. Give him or her a copy of the "Capernaum Skit." Explain that while the rest of the kids are readying the room for Jesus to come, he or she can put on a Bible-times costume.

Say: **If you were to inspect these envelopes, you'd find that they're blank and so are the papers inside them. Please take an envelope and a pencil and set them on the floor in front of you. This is going to be fun, but you're going to have to think really hard before you write anything down.**

Here's the picture. Have you ever seen the end of a really big football game on TV when they show the winning quarterback? A voice names the quarterback and says, "You just won the Super Bowl. What are you going to do next?" Then they show a shot of the quarterback as he shouts, "I'm goin' to Disneyland!" Or have you seen a commercial on TV that shows someone stepping outside the front door to receive a check for one million dollars?

Well, we're going to set up that kind of activity for you— only it's all made-up, of course.

In your wildest dreams, suppose you could win something like a fancy trip or a large amount of money. What exactly would you like to win? Think very, very carefully about this before you write anything. Suppose, for instance, your trip could take you back in time, or your amount of money could be enough to cure a disease, or you could bring fresh water to everyone who lives in Africa. Suppose you could buy a house for everyone who doesn't have one. Or maybe you'd just like to go to Disneyland!

Form pairs and work on this together. If you need help writing, find a partner who can help you.

The first thing to write is: It's Sunday and I won... Then write what your wonderful prize is. We'll take about three minutes for you to form pairs and complete your papers. Then tuck them back in your envelopes, seal your envelopes shut, and drop them in my box.

Walk among pairs as they complete this activity, offering suggestions to any pairs who seem to be struggling. For fun, fill out a paper of your own and drop your envelope into the box.

Prep Box

Before class, scatter pencils and blank envelopes with blanks sheets of paper tucked inside on the floor of your room where you usually gather for stories.

All Together Now

Gather kids around the box with a great air of excitement.

Say: **I can't wait to see what everyone won! When I open an envelope and read it, let's see if we can guess who wrote the winning prize and give that person a big cheer!**

With great drama, open each envelope and read, **It's Sunday and I won...** Have kids cheer loudly, and then let kids guess who chose that prize.

Say: **The amazing thing is that Jesus could create the kind of excitement we're talking about just by walking into a town. No kidding. When Jesus showed up, people knew that things they'd never dared to dream about were going to happen. That's because ★ *Jesus' teachings and healings are amazing.* The news would spread quickly and everyone would run to see Jesus—what would he say? What would he do?**

Let's find out!

BIBLE EXPLORATION

. . . .

Jesus Is Here (Luke 4:31-44; 5:12-16)

Say: **Before Jesus arrives, we need to set the stage. I have three tasks for you. First, we're in the town of Capernaum. We need someone to make a sign that tells everyone that this is Capernaum.** Pause.

Now we need two sick people. First, let's have someone with a terrible skin disease called leprosy. This person must be OK with people wrapping his or her arms with cloths and using a washable red marker to make sores on the hands and face. There's a box of fabric scraps for bandages and some washable markers. We need three people to do that job. Pause.

Then let's have an older lady with a terrible fever. You'll need to put a shawl over her head and make a bed for her on the floor. If she'll let you, you can make wrinkles on her face with washable markers, too. We need two people to do this job. Pause.

As kids work on creating a person with leprosy, give that person the index card that says, "Lord, if you are willing, you can make me clean." Explain that he or she will say this line when Jesus comes to him or her. Go over the line with him or her a few times to make sure the child has it down.

Prep Box

Set out a box with shawls for Bible-times head-coverings, strips of cloth for bandages, blankets to make a bed on the floor, and washable markers. Also have ready the index card with the leper's statement and some paper for a sign.

If you have other items to create the look of a Bible-times village, such as potted palms, clay jars, foam rocks, or striped blankets, have kids set those out as well, forming a "road" through the village.

When all the jobs are done, say: **Hurry, hurry, everybody, because Jesus is just about to come to town! Pass the word to everyone! We don't want anyone to miss the chance to see Jesus! Come on! Let's put the person with leprosy way out to be the first person Jesus will meet. But wait—we don't want any of the rest of us to get close or we might catch that terrible disease. Be sure you don't touch that person.**

We're going to put on a little impromptu skit as Jesus arrives. Only our "Jesus" actor and I know the lines, so the rest of you have to watch me for your cues about what to do.

Are you ready? Let's see what happens when Jesus visits Capernaum!

Note: Begin the "Capernaum Skit" here. This will continue and finish your Bible story.

Once kids have finished telling everyone that Jesus is here, gather them in a group in the middle of your "Capernaum."

Thank everyone for participating in the skit. Ask:

• **What did you learn about Jesus in our skit?**

• **Explain whether you think Jesus is more of a teacher or a healer—and why.**

• **Tell about a time you or someone you know was healed.**

Say: **When Jesus began his ministry in Capernaum, he became famous in a time before the Internet and television. But he didn't get famous for doing tricks or stunts. Jesus was doing real miracles that changed real people's lives.** ★*Jesus' teachings and healings were amazing.* **And the good news is that** ★*Jesus' teachings and healings are still amazing* **today. Let's take a look at how we know Jesus is still here with us.**

LIFE APPLICATION
....

Jesus Is Here Pop-Up

Say: ★*Jesus' teachings and healings are amazing.* **But Jesus doesn't come walking into town like he did when he**

All Together Now

Capernaum Skit

Jesus and Teacher approach the person with leprosy.

LEPER: **Lord, if you are willing, you can make me clean.**

JESUS: **I am willing.**

Jesus touches Leper tenderly on the head and then takes one hand.

JESUS: **Be clean!**

Teacher encourages Leper to look at his or her hands and then to stand up and shout, "I'm clean! I'm clean!"

Jesus moves on into town; speaking to the people who've gathered.

JESUS: *(loudly)* **I bring good news of the kingdom of God! This is the year of the Lord's favor!**

TEACHER: **Did you hear? Jesus healed the person with leprosy just up the road! He even *touched* the person!**

Teacher encourages townspeople to be amazed.

TEACHER: **Jesus, can you help Peter's mother-in-law? She's sick with a terrible fever.**

JESUS: **Take me to her.**

TEACHER: **Everyone, show Jesus the sick old woman.**

Jesus kneels by the old woman and takes her hand.

Teacher signals the old woman to rise and to rejoice that she's well.

TEACHER: **Look! Peter's mother-in-law is healed! Rejoice with me, everyone! Our dear sister was very sick, but now she's well!**

Teacher leads kids in a celebratory circle, moving around the healed woman.

Jesus stands by smiling.

TEACHER: *(breaking up the circle)* **Wait! Do any of you have sick relatives or friends? Hurry and bring them to Jesus! Tell everybody! Jesus is here! Go! Go! Tell everyone! Jesus is here!**

Published in *All Together Now, Volume 2* by Group Publishing, Inc., 1515 Cascade Ave., Loveland, CO 80538.

73

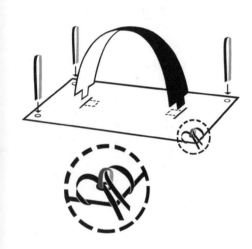

lived on earth. People don't flock to the hillsides to hear him speak. He doesn't have crowds of people waving palm leaves at him.

When we put our faith in Jesus, he lives in our *hearts*. When lots of us who believe in Jesus come together, we each bring some of Jesus with us. When we worship Jesus, he's with us! Jesus himself said, "And be sure of this: I am with you always, even to the end of the age" (Matthew 28:20).

Now that's something we want to celebrate! Let's do it with a special pop-up!

Guide kids to the craft table where you've set out the supplies.

Say: **This pop-up will give you a way to talk about today's lesson at home with your families and friends. And it makes a pretty cool centerpiece for your dining room table. It's quick and easy to make, so let's get poppin'!**

You'll find step-by-step instructions for assembly printed on the handout. If you have plenty of time, you may want to let kids decorate the pop-up further with markers, glitter glue, or other items of choice.

As kids finish, have them straighten the craft area and join you in a discussion circle.

COMMITMENT
....

Family Discussion

Say: **Let's think of all the different ways we could use these pop-ups to start a discussion about Jesus at home.** Let kids contribute several ideas.

Say: **Let's talk through the questions on the handout.**
Ask:
• **What happened when Jesus visited a town?**
• **Why were people so happy to see Jesus?**
Say: ★ *Jesus' teachings and healings are amazing.* **Today we've looked at just a few moments in Jesus' amazing life and teachings. I encourage you to keep reading your Bible to see how Jesus can speak to you in your own life and to feel his presence with you every day.**

Optional: If you have extra time, you may wish to sing a favorite worship song to Jesus.

All Together Now

Jesus Is Here
Pop-Up

1. Cut out the base and the pop-up.
2. Fold the tabs at the end of the pop-up back and forth; then slide them through the slits in the base.
3. Secure the tabs with transparent tape on the back side of the base.
4. Punch holes in the circles near the corners. Tie ribbons through the holes (see illustration on page 74.).

Why were people so happy to see Jesus?

What happened when Jesus visited a town?

JESUS IS HERE

Closing Prayer

Say: **Let's close in prayer.**

Dear Jesus, it would've been cool to be around when you lived on earth, to see the way you loved people. Thank you for leaving us your Word so we can know ★ *your teachings and healings are amazing.* **Most of all, thank you for your promise to be with us now. Our hearts are filled with love for you! In your name, amen.**

A Roman Officer Meets Jesus

LESSON AIM

To encourage kids to realize that ★ *we can put our faith in Jesus' power.*

OBJECTIVES

Kids will

✓ make a Roman soldier's costume from a paper bag,

✓ participate in a Readers Theater about the Roman centurion's encounter with Jesus,

✓ enjoy "Faith Floats" as they discuss what happens when faith meets Jesus' power, and

✓ make "Faith Floats" invitations to take home to their families.

BIBLE BASIS

 Matthew 8:5-13

The first thing to notice about this Scripture is that this is one of the first one-on-one encounters Jesus had with a Gentile, or someone who was a non-Jew. Prior to this point, Jesus' ministry had been limited primarily to his own people, the Jews. The other thing to note is that the encounter was with a centurion, an officer in the Roman army.

Centurions, officers who oversaw 100 Roman soldiers, were the backbone of the Roman army. It was their job to discipline, maintain training and fitness, and lead from the front

You'll need...

☐ 1 large plain brown paper grocery bag for each child plus a few extras, prepared as explained on page 80

☐ scissors

☐ staplers

☐ hole punch

☐ large brads

☐ masking tape

☐ name tags hung on yarn: Jesus, Centurion, Narrator

☐ 2 copies of the "Readers Theater" script (pp. 82-83)

☐ orange soda*

☐ orange sherbet*

☐ ice cream scoop

☐ clear plastic cups

☐ plastic tablecloth

☐ colorful straws

☐ plastic spoons

☐ wet wipes

☐ small, colorful napkins

☐ copies of the "Faith Floats" handout (p. 85)

☐ craft knife

☐ optional: camera

* Always check for allergies before serving snacks.

in war. Centurions worked their way up through the ranks by acts of courage that distinguished them from their peers.

To Jews, centurions represented the hated and unclean Roman Empire, which had invaded and now occupied the holy land of Israel. Thus, this encounter would've been suspect to Jewish listeners as unclean on top of unclean: The Roman officer was not just unclean because he was a Gentile, but even more so because he was perceived to be an enemy of God.

We know that many Romans looked down on the Jews as second-class citizens or grew increasingly annoyed by their perceived troublemaking. They also found Jewish dietary laws to be strange. When he speaks to Jesus, the faith he shows makes it clear that the centurion was truly a God-seeker.

The centurion asked for healing for his servant. It's remarkable that a respected Roman officer would bear such concern for a suffering servant. It's difficult for people today to get our minds around the attitude that existed toward slaves in the Roman era. For many slaveholders, slaves were nothing more than disposable tools that talked. There was little regard for their comfort, their feelings, or their human needs.

So for a soldier whose life was invested in hardening himself and his soldiers for battle to display such compassion for a servant was remarkable. For this soldier to humble himself to the point of asking for help from a wandering rabbi in an insignificant conquered land was unheard of. This kind of thing just *did not happen.*

Now comes the kicker. How much of Jesus' teaching and miracles had the centurion actually witnessed? Likely, few to none. He couldn't exactly mingle with crowds unnoticed. He must've known of Jesus' works primarily through word of mouth. Yet, based on what he'd heard, the centurion had so much faith in this young, charismatic rabbi that he was certain Jesus could heal his suffering servant without so much as visiting his house, but merely by willing that it be done.

Jesus himself was amazed at this level of faith. In turn he made a shocking statement to his Jewish listeners—that many sons and daughters of Abraham would be left out in the place of weeping and gnashing of teeth while Gentiles like this centurion would sit and feast with Abraham, Isaac, and Jacob in the kingdom of heaven. This was news to the Jews. It was indeed the first time any of them had heard that their heritage alone wouldn't get them into the kingdom of heaven. A whole group of people must've sucked in their breath in surprise.

All Together Now

Then Jesus turned his attention back to the centurion. " 'Go back home. Because you believed, it has happened.' And the young servant was healed that same hour" (Matthew 8:13).

Chills. Drama. Extraordinary faith—from a Gentile! Jesus was emerging as not just another teacher, but as an entirely new phenomenon.

 Isaiah 11:10

God chose Abraham in his old age to become the patriarch of the Hebrew people. God and Abraham entered into a covenant: God was to be the God of the Hebrews, and they were to be his people. Many more covenants were made, including one with King David that his line would rule Israel forever (2 Samuel 7:16). For centuries the Jews thought of themselves as unique heirs to God's kingdom by their heritage alone.

Sadly, the Jews turned out to be an unruly, rebellious people who didn't set their eyes on God's holiness or live by his laws the way God intended. As a result, God allowed his people to fall into the hands of conquerors. However, God wasn't "done" with the people. Isaiah 11:10 prophesized that an "heir to David's throne" would serve as a "banner of salvation to all the world" and that all "nations will rally to him." Jesus was this heir. Jesus brought the Gospel to the Jews first, but ultimately also to the Gentiles.

UNDERSTANDING YOUR KIDS

There may come a day when ~~many of~~ you your kids will sit in classes where professors casually explain away Jesus' miracles as if the actions were nothing out of the ordinary at all. I remember with clarity how shocked and stripped of something precious I felt when that first happened to me. I was mature enough in my walk with Jesus to consider for a while and then say, *no—by faith I choose to believe that Jesus did what Scripture said he did.* ★ *We can put our faith in Jesus' power.* And that's where I still stand.

Most people will make these important faith decisions by age 12 and then cling to their early beliefs for the rest of their lives. ~~You~~ have the great privilege of molding kids' faith during these impressionable years. Of helping them develop the kind of faith in Jesus that the centurion had. Remember always that you're making a profound difference in the lives of the kids you teach!

THE LESSON »

Armor Up!

Welcome kids.

Say: **Today a *Roman officer* is going to invade our room. The nation of Israel had been conquered by the Roman Empire, and so Roman soldiers were stationed in Israel during Jesus' lifetime. They were there to keep peace and order.**

Do you think a Roman soldier talking to Jesus might be a good thing or a bad thing? Just take a guess. Pause.

We'll find out soon enough! But let's get ready first. You see, this wasn't just any Roman soldier. This was a centurion—a leader of 100 men. The famous Roman legions were based on groups of 100 men. So centurions played a big role in holding the Roman army together.

I guess we'd better be in uniform before this centurion shows up. Let's make our uniforms.

Lead kids to the craft table where you've set out the supplies.

Demonstrate how to cut out the sides of the bags down to the second folds, according to illustration B.

Show kids how to cut the pieces of each of the sides they've just cut away into five strips. It doesn't matter if the strips aren't exactly the same width (see illustration B).

Have an adult assistant or older child work with each child to staple a set of strips along a strap as shown. Then repeat with the other strap (see illustration B).

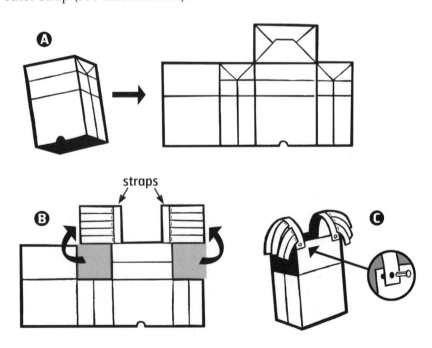

Prep Box

Before class, prepare a paper grocery bag for each child as follows:

Cut from top to bottom at a side near the back seam. Continue cutting out the bottom until it's only attached to the front part of the bag (see illustration A).

Cut away the bottom, leaving two- to three-inch straps on each side (see illustration B).

Use staples to reinforce where the straps join the bag.

Then set out on a craft table the prepared bags, scissors, hole punch, staplers, brads, and masking tape.

All Together Now

For the next step, have kids try on their uniforms. Have an adult hole punch through the top of each strap and mark the place on the back of the uniform where the straps should attach. Kids can hole punch the marked spots on their uniforms and then attach the straps to the uniforms with large brads (see illustration C).

Say: **Nice work, everyone! Now you're ready to get all suited up. Slip your head through the straps and then I'll close the sides loosely with a couple of strips of masking tape.**

We're about to learn more about the centurion who met Jesus. Like the centurion, ★ *we can put our faith in Jesus' power.*

Teacher Tip

This would be a great time to assemble your "troops" for a group photo to e-mail to kids' homes later in the week.

BIBLE EXPLORATION

. . . .

Amazing Faith (Matthew 8:5-13)

Say: **Today we're going to do a Readers Theater presentation of what happened to Jesus—straight from the Bible. Some of you will read what happened, and the rest of you get to act out the cues our readers give you, so listen closely.**

Choose fluent, expressive readers to read the parts of the Centurion and Jesus, and give them copies of the "Readers Theater" script. Help the reader for Jesus remove his or her uniform. When you place the name tag around the Centurion's neck, have the rest of the kids be "soldiers" as they stand and salute him. Then have them bow before Jesus and say, "Rabbi." You will play the part of the Narrator. Be prepared to direct the kids in certain actions.

Matthew 8:5-13

NARRATOR: **When Jesus returned to Capernaum, a Roman officer came and pleaded with him.**

(Point to the Centurion.)

CENTURION: **Lord, my young servant lies in bed, paralyzed and in terrible pain.**

NARRATOR: **Jesus said:**

(Point to Jesus.)

JESUS: **I will come and heal him.**

NARRATOR: **But the officer said:**

(Point to the Centurion.)

CENTURION: **Lord, I am not worthy to have you come into my home. Just say the word from where you are, and my servant will be healed. I know this because I am under the authority of my superior officers, and I have authority over my soldiers. I only need to say, "Go," and they go, or "Come," and they come. And if I say to my slaves, "Do this," they do it.**

NARRATOR: **When Jesus heard this, he was amazed. Turning to those who were following him, he said:**

(Point to Jesus.)

JESUS: **I tell you the truth, I haven't seen faith like this in all Israel! And I tell you this, that many Gentiles will come from all over the world—from east and west—and sit down with Abraham, Isaac, and Jacob at the feast in the Kingdom of Heaven. But many Israelites—those for whom the Kingdom was prepared—will be thrown into outer darkness, where there will be weeping and gnashing of teeth.**

NARRATOR: **Then Jesus said to the Roman officer:**

(Point to Jesus.)

JESUS: **Go back home. Because you believed, it has happened.**

All Together Now

NARRATOR: **And the young servant was healed that same hour.**

NARRATOR: **Israel had been conquered by the Roman Empire. The Roman soldiers were there to enforce Roman law and keep the peace. For most Jews, Romans were the enemy. When a Roman officer came to Jesus and asked for help, there must've been a big gasp of surprise from the crowd.**

(Point to the rest of the kids and encourage them to let out a big gasp.)

Another surprise was that the Roman officer asked Jesus to heal his servant. That servant was really a slave. Most of the time, Romans didn't even think of their slaves as people, much less care when they got sick.

(Have kids pretend to cough into their fists.)

So we have a Roman centurion who may not have even seen Jesus before. It's possible that he'd just heard of Jesus' teaching and of his miracles. We don't know for sure. Yet the centurion came to Jesus for help in broad daylight in Jesus' own home base of Capernaum.

(Point to the Centurion and have him or her pretend to knock on an invisible door.)

Jesus was so amazed at the centurion's faith that he stopped right there and preached a little sermon to everyone who was watching. Jesus said that he hadn't seen such faith among all the Jewish people. And he added that some non-Jews—like this centurion—would someday feast in heaven, while Jews without faith would not. That was a huge shock to everyone who was listening to Jesus. They thought that just belonging to the right family was enough to get them to heaven. But no! Jesus used the Roman centurion as an example of a man of faith who would be in heaven someday. That kind of talk turned everyone upside down! Jesus was looking for people with faith.

(Have kids, including the Centurion, fold their hands and bow their heads as if in prayer.)

The centurion's servant was healed even though Jesus wasn't even close by! The centurion accepted Jesus' authority and put his faith in Jesus' power. ★ *We, too, can put our faith in Jesus' power.*

Permission to photocopy this handout granted for local church use. Copyright © Lois Keffer. Published in *All Together Now, Volume 2* by Group Publishing, Inc., 1515 Cascade Ave., Loveland, CO 80538.

Say: **Let's give our readers some applause. I'm glad I serve a Savior who has all the power in the universe, whether physically he's here in the room or far away.**

Let's move on to see how we can apply that truth in our lives.

LIFE APPLICATION

Faith Floats!

Lead kids to the table where the ingredients are laid out.

Say: **You must be tired and thirsty after all the work you put into your uniforms *and* participating in our Readers Theater. That's why I'm treating you to** (uncover the ingredients) **faith floats!**

Let's remember that (plop a scoop of sherbet into a cup) **Jesus has all the power in the universe. When that power meets the kind of faith the centurion had,** (quickly swish soda into the cup)**, anything can happen! Blind people see, those with leprosy get healthy, and a servant can be healed from miles away! Jesus' power bubbles over and faith floats—don't you love it?**

Now come pour some bubbling faith into your own floats. Then we'll make faith floats invitations for you to take home to your families.

Supervise kids as they scoop sherbet and pour soda into their own cups. Remind them that the sherbet represents Jesus' power, while the soda represents faith like the centurion's. As kids finish enjoying their floats, say:

Jesus is all-powerful. It's a huge comfort to know ★ *we can put our faith in Jesus' power.* Your floats symbolize this truth. Sherbet by itself is good, but when soda is added, it becomes a bubbling sensation. Let's move on to see how we can commit to Jesus' power.

Pass out wet wipes to kids, and let them clean up.

COMMITMENT

Faith Floats Invitations

Direct kids to the craft table where you've set out the supplies.

Prep Box

Place orange soda, orange sherbet, an ice cream scoop, straws, plastic spoons, and clear plastic cups on a table; then cover everything with a plastic tablecloth.

Prep Box

Before class, set out on a craft table the "Faith Floats" handouts; small, colorful napkins; and straws. Open the slits in the handouts with a craft knife.

All Together Now

Faith Floats!

1. Cut out the oval invitation to take to your family.
2. Your teacher has cut the two slits with a craft knife.
3. Tuck a colorful napkin and a straw into the slits.
4. Take the invitation home. Have fun making faith floats and talking about the story of the centurion and Jesus with your family!

Faith Floats

Read the story of Jesus and the centurion in Matthew 8:5-13. Make faith floats with 1 scoop of sherbet in each cup to represent Jesus' power. Add soda to represent the centurion's faith. Watch what happens!

- What was so amazing about the centurion's faith?
- When have we really trusted in Jesus as a family?
- When has Jesus shown his power in our lives?
- Do you think Jesus would help us have more faith if we asked him?

Family Prayer

Dear Jesus,

We believe that you came to show us the way to God. Please help our faith in you grow stronger and stronger.

Amen.

Show kids how to open the napkin and then pull it down from the center into several nice points. They can weave the top point through the slits and spread out the bottom to give the invitation a nice look and then top it all off by sliding a colorful straw into the slits as well. You may wish to trim the length of the straw a bit.

Say: **Share your invitations with your families.**

Check out the discussion questions on your invitations. Talk about these questions with your family. Have fun! I'll bet your families will love learning from the Bible as much as we do.

CLOSING

Faith Like a Centurion

I hope you'll take your uniform home, fold it neatly, and keep it for times you especially need your faith to be strong. Then you can slip it on and pray for God to give you faith like the centurion had.

Have kids bend their elbows, join fists in the air, and shout: ★ *We can put our faith in Jesus' power!*

Before kids leave, you may want to help them slip off their uniforms and fold them neatly to carry home with their "Faith Floats" invitations.

Jesus and the Tax Collector

LESSON AIM

To help kids realize that ★ *Jesus' love can change anyone.*

OBJECTIVES

Kids will

✓ play a face-making game,

✓ participate in an interactive story about Jesus calling Matthew to follow him,

✓ grapple with how Jesus changes people's hearts,

✓ create a pop-up card about how Jesus changes people, and

✓ pray to see past people's behavior and consider what's in their hearts.

BIBLE BASIS

 Matthew 9:9-13

Matthew, the tax collector: Habitual cheater. Collaborator with the Romans. Double-dipper. Turncoat. Someone who enriched himself at the expense of the poor.

Have you gotten a bad taste in your mouth about Matthew yet? If so, you would've had plenty of company in Jesus' time.

Matthew was a Jewish man who'd chosen a job that made him almost as hated as the Romans: tax collector. He was down there with harlots and thieves. And no doubt he felt it. A

You'll need...

☐ 3 paper plates labeled 1 to 3

☐ several coins, the more the better (optional: toy gold and silver coins)

☐ expensive-looking scarf or robe

☐ plate of breakfast treats*

☐ small box of doughnut holes*

☐ napkins

☐ Bible

☐ copies of the "Jesus' Love Can Change Anyone" handout (p. 96)

☐ scissors

☐ optional: glue sticks

* Always check for allergies before serving snacks.

sea of angry faces and turned backs greeted him wherever he went. He was the lowest of the low and he knew it.

The Romans let the tax collector jobs go to the highest bidder. The commission? Whatever else they could squeeze out of people to keep for themselves.

We think ourselves tax-weary in modern times, but in Bible times there were taxes required for everything from roads to animals to the Temple. Now imagine you're a typical Galilean peasant. If you saw wealthy Matthew buying all of the best goods at the market while you could barely dress and feed your family, you wouldn't be happy with him. Truly, the people of Capernaum had plenty of reason to take issue with this man of their own blood who openly worked with the Romans and made their own lives harder.

For Matthew, was the house full of money worth the lifetime of rejection? Maybe not. With his tax booth situated where it was (in the public forum), he'd probably had plenty of exposure to Jesus' teaching. And, oh! How sweet it must have sounded! A loving God. Repentance. Forgiveness. A chance to start over.

Like anyone would forgive *him*!

So imagine Matthew's utter shock when Jesus looked at him sitting in his tax collector's booth and said, "Follow me." Matthew got up and followed him. And Capernaum was turned on its ear.

Are there difficult people in your life? What if Jesus were to confront them and say, "Follow me"? And what if they responded? Kind of turns reality on its ear, doesn't it?

But that's why Jesus came: to seek and to save those who are lost. Jesus' love can change anyone.

 **Hosea 6:6**

If you've never read the short prophetic book of Hosea, this is a great time to glance through it. Why Hosea? Why now?

Jesus ended up having dinner at Matthew's house. Matthew was so excited about his newfound life in Jesus that he invited several fellow tax collectors, probably so they could hear the good news from Jesus himself.

The Pharisees, the righteous people of the day, had plenty to say about Jesus dining in such company. It was unheard of for a rabbi to enter into fellowship with such an unseemly lot of people. Jesus replied to their criticism with these words: "Healthy people don't need a doctor—sick people do." Then Jesus quoted from Hosea 6:6: "Now go and learn the meaning of this Scripture: 'I want you to show mercy, not offer sacrifices.' For I have come to call not those

All Together Now

who think they are righteous, but those who know they are sinners" (Matthew 9:12-13).

More than the other Gospel writers, Matthew knew the sting of the Pharisees' cynical disregard. Their self-righteousness was no more honest and authentic than his complete lack of righteousness. So in quoting Jesus here, Matthew included a little tidbit which implied that the Pharisees were every bit as unfaithful to God as the Israelites of old.

UNDERSTANDING YOUR KIDS

Headlines tell story after story of the pain of being the outcast. Some adults, like Matthew, make poor choices that lead to their own pain, suffering, and social isolation. But children? The choice is not usually theirs, and the pain is magnified.

Sometimes it's just the lack of having the "it" factor. Sometimes it's a learning disability, an irregular facial feature, or painful shyness. Don't you just ache for the child in your group who, despite your encouraging efforts, has trouble meshing with the rest of the kids?

Children can be unwittingly cruel to a child they're used to seeing in the role of outcast. They begin to assume that less social children are used to being shunned when others choose teams or partners or that they somehow grow immune to giggles and sideways comments.

Use this lesson about Matthew to teach kids that everyone wants to be "found" the way Jesus found Matthew, and that it takes extraordinary love to look outside their group of friends to share Jesus' love.

THE LESSON »

Such Faces!

Welcome kids enthusiastically. Have them form a circle, and invite them to "warm up" their faces.

Say: **We're going to use our faces a lot in our opening activity, so please join me by standing in a circle and we'll practice getting our faces all nice and rubbery.**

Lead kids in funny-looking facial warm-ups by dropping your jaw and wiggling it around, pushing your cheeks up as high as they'll go, wiggling your ears all around, putting your hands on the sides of your head and stretching your face back, raising your eyebrows and rolling your eyes around, and wrinkling your nose and wiggling it. Add other "facial stretches" as you think of them.

This little exercise should get everyone giggling!

Say: **I can see that your faces have a lot of potential!**

Now I'm going to call out a face to make. When I do, hold that face until you've shown it to everyone in the circle. In other words, don't just look at me. Make your face and look around at everyone. By the way, you may use your hands as props, but you may *not* use sound effects. And whatever you do, don't laugh!

Call out these faces, allowing plenty of time for kids to enjoy the faces other kids in the circle make:

- ✓ **like you've just heard shocking news**
- ✓ **like you just swallowed a giant gumball whole**
- ✓ **like you've got a giant toothache**
- ✓ **like you think you're better than everyone else**
- ✓ **like you just got stung by a bee**
- ✓ **like your dream just came true**
- ✓ **like someone just hurt your feelings**

Say: **Give each other a round of applause for those great faces!**

Ask:

- **What were some of your favorite faces?**

Encourage kids to point out the great faces others made, and also point out kids' faces you liked.

Say: **We're going to encounter several of those faces today when we hear about the time Jesus met someone the other people hated. Later on, we'll explore the feelings people had—and you may be surprised by who felt what.**

All Together Now

You may even be surprised by your own feelings. Most importantly, we'll look at how ★*Jesus' love can change anyone*. Hmm. This sounds pretty interesting. Let's get started!

BIBLE EXPLORATION
....

Jesus and the Tax Collector (Matthew 9:9-13)

Have kids stand as you spread the numbered plates across the floor.

Say: **I'm going to name some characteristics of a person. If what I say would help you really like that person, go stand by plate number 3. If what I say might make you dislike that person, stand by plate number 1. If it wouldn't make any difference, stand by plate number 2. Are you ready?**

Pause after reading each characteristic to let kids respond.

✓ **Cheats to make himself rich while other people grow poor.**

✓ **Betrays his own country.**

✓ **Takes more than everyone else gets.**

Say: **How's our person doing so far? Not so well, huh? I'm not surprised. Let's gather in a circle and I'll tell you more about this person. I want you to remember the faces we just practiced making, and as I tell you about the person, go ahead and make the face that best fits how you feel about him. His name is Matthew and he's a...**(gather the children close so you can whisper it) **tax collector** (exaggerate a disgusted look for kids to emulate). **He collected taxes for the hated...** (gather the children close once again and make a face) **Romans.**

You see, even though Matthew was a Jew, he turned on his own people and worked for the Romans. Everybody say "eew" with me when I put my thumb down. (thumb down) **EEW! The other Jews considered him as bad as a thief. In fact, he was a thief!** (thumb down and angry face) **EEW! The taxes that the Romans charged people made them poor.** (thumb down and sad face) **EEW! Then the tax collectors collected as much for themselves as they wanted to.** (thumb down and angry face) **EEW! So while the people of Israel grew poorer and poorer, the tax collectors got richer and richer.** (thumb down and disgusted face) **EEW! It was unfair! It was**

(handwritten note:) like-smile dislike-frown no difference normal

awful! It was downright terrible! (thumb down and angry face) EEW!

Of course the tax collectors always wore the finest garments. Drape a fine scarf or robe around one of the kids in the circle. They always had bags full of money. Spill the coins in front of the same child. When they went to the market they always bought the finest food (place a plate of breakfast treats, such as doughnuts, in front of your tax collector—heaping amounts if possible), while everyone else bought barely enough to feed their families (place one doughnut hole on a napkin in front of everyone else).

Ask:

• Describe how you feel about the amount of food you have compared with what the tax collector has.

• Describe what it's like when someone takes more than you.

Say: Of course, no one wanted to be friends with the tax collectors. They were traitors, cheats, and thieves! So when a tax collector came into town, everyone else turned away. Lead the rest of the children in turning away from the child pretending to be the tax collector.

Say: Everyone, that is, but Jesus! Imagine everyone's surprise when Jesus walked by the tax booth where Matthew worked and said to Matthew, "Follow me."

Jesus used the words "follow me" to call his disciples— his closest friends. People who were traveling with Jesus must've thought they heard wrong. Matthew himself must've been startled. But only for a moment, because he jumped right up and followed Jesus.

Wait a minute!

Ask:

• What do you think about Jesus calling someone like Matthew, who people thought was a "loser," to be a disciple?

Let's check it out in the Bible.

Ask a willing child to read Matthew 9:9-11 aloud.

Say: Jesus surprised everyone by choosing a tax collector to be his disciple.

As the Bible says, a little later Jesus went to Matthew's home to have dinner. Matthew was so excited that he invited his tax collector friends to meet Jesus.

Ask:

• What do you think Jesus might have said to them?

All Together Now

• Tell whether it seems fair to you that Jesus reached out to the "bad" people rather than the "good" ones.

• What do Jesus' actions toward Matthew say about Jesus?

Say: **Let's keep making our faces to show how we feel about what happened. Tax collectors never expected to have a second chance to be accepted back by the people of God. They never expected to hear about a loving God. They never expected to have Jesus set foot in one of their homes and eat with them.** Pause for kids to make a face. **For Matthew, it must have seemed like a dream come true. He could leave his old life of sin, be forgiven by Jesus, and start a new life being Jesus' disciple. It was almost too good to be true.** Pause for kids to make a face. **His heart must've flooded with joy.** Pause for kids to make a face. **This most despised person was welcomed into the kingdom of God. Let's join hands and jump for joy to express Matthew's happiness.** Lead kids in jumping for joy.

Say: **Of course the townspeople were surprised** (pause for kids to make a face), **but they'd been surprised by Jesus many times before. Then there were the Pharisees. They thought they were better at keeping God's law than anyone else. Remember that face—thinking that you're better than anyone else? Let's make it again.** Pause for kids to make a face. **That's right! The Pharisees looked in Matthew's house and saw Jesus eating with a bunch of sinners! They looked down their long noses and said, "What's he doing eating with** *them*?" Pause for kids to make a face.

Jesus had a ready answer: " 'Healthy people don't need a doctor—sick people do.' Then he added, 'Now go and learn the meaning of this Scripture: "I want you to show mercy, not offer sacrifices." For I have come to call not those who think they are righteous, but those who know they are sinners' " (Matthew 9:12-13).

I don't know how long it took before people started smiling (pause for kids to make a face) **at Matthew rather than turning away from him. It probably happened little by little. But Matthew knew that one person had seen past his riches and into his hurting heart.** Pause for kids to make a face. **That person was...** Let the kids finish by saying, "Jesus."

Now, our tax collector will share the breakfast riches with everyone while we discuss what Jesus did. Pause for kids to make a face.

Ask:

- **What surprises you most about Jesus choosing Matthew as a disciple?**

- **Based on what you know about Jesus, what are reasons you think he may have chosen Matthew?**

- **Tell whether you think Matthew deserved to be Jesus' disciple—and why or why not.**

Say: **The truth is, none of us really deserves to be Jesus' disciple, because we're all sinners, meaning we're all guilty of not doing what God wants us to do. Matthew's sins were obvious. The coldhearted Pharisees were sinners, too, because of their lack of love. But Jesus loves everyone. In the end, no matter what,** ★ *Jesus' love can change anyone.*

LIFE APPLICATION
....

Change Goes Both Ways

Say: **Jesus saw past the nasty person Matthew was on the outside right into his hurting heart. Wouldn't it be cool if we could see people the same way Jesus does?**

Take a moment to think of someone who isn't particularly nice to you.

Ask:

- **If you could look past the outside, what do you think you might find in that person's heart?**

Say: **Sometimes it's hard to see how some people could end up being followers of Jesus. Matthew was fortunate enough to be face to face with Jesus.**

Ask:

- **Who are some people you know who need to meet Jesus?**

Say: **Wouldn't it be something if someone saw Jesus in you** (point to a child) **or you** (point to another child) **or you** (point to a third child])**?**

Say: ★ *Jesus' love can change anyone.* **Jesus wants us to see people's hurting hearts rather than their outside behavior. None of us is perfect, and we all need to know Jesus—and I have a way to help you introduce him to others!**

All Together Now

COMMITMENT

Jesus' Love Can Change Anyone

Gather kids at the craft table where you've set out the supplies.
Say: There's nothing like a little pop-up to amaze everyone with your crafting skills *and* share today's important Bible story!

Lead kids through the following steps to complete the pop-up card.

- ✓ Fold the card in half on the dotted line. Make sure the corners of the card line up. Crease the fold well.

- ✓ While the card is still folded, trim away the edges of the card on the solid line.

- ✓ Open the card and fold it in half the long way so the fold runs exactly through the center of the hearts. To start the fold, pinch the center of each heart and the X where the hearts intersect. Crease the fold well.

- ✓ While the card is still folded, cut the hearts on the solid line. Then fold the hearts back and forth on the dotted lines. Crease the folds well.

- ✓ Finally, open the card and fold it in half horizontally again.

- ✓ As you close the card, pull the pop-up hearts forward. Each time you open and close the card, the hearts will pop up! (Optional: If you wish, rub a dot of glue stick on the point of the cut-out behind each heart and press it to the back of the card to hold it in place.)

As kids work, offer assistance as needed. Ask questions such as "When will you share this card with your family?" or "Tell about the special person you plan to share this card with."

As kids finish, invite them to help other kids who are still working or to begin cleaning up the craft area.

Prep Box

Set out copies of the "Jesus' Love Can Change Anyone" handout," scissors, and glue sticks (optional). Before class, make a completed pop-up card to show kids as a sample.

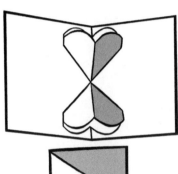

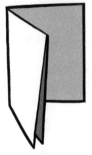

Jesus Calls Matthew

[9] As Jesus was walking along, he saw a man named Matthew sitting at his tax collector's booth. "Follow me and be my disciple," Jesus said to him. So Matthew got up and followed him.

[10] Later, Matthew invited Jesus and his disciples to his home as dinner guests, along with many tax collectors and other disreputable sinners. [11] But when the Pharisees saw this, they asked his disciples, "Why does your teacher eat with such scum?"

[12] When Jesus heard this, he said, "Healthy people don't need a doctor—sick people do." [13] Then he added, "Now go and learn the meaning of this Scripture: 'I want you to show mercy, not offer sacrifices.' For I have come to call not those who think they are righteous, but those who know they are sinners."

Matthew 9:9-13

CLOSING

Change Our Hearts, O Lord

Form a circle for closing prayer.

Say: **I'm going to pray part of this prayer out loud, but I'll stop in two places for you to fill in your own private prayers. Then, after a few seconds, I'll go on. Please pray with me.**

Dear Lord, we thank you for this wonderful story of Matthew, the hated man whose hurting heart only you could see. Right now we're thinking of people like that in our lives. Please help us see past their behavior and into their hurting hearts like you would, Jesus. Pause. **And Lord, we ask you to make us a little bit more like you every day so when people see us they will see Jesus also. We humbly ask you to change our hearts, too.** Pause. **We love you more than words can tell, Jesus. Thank you for being our Savior and Lord. Amen.**

Jesus and the Humongous Picnic

Lesson 9

LESSON AIM

To help kids trust that ★*Jesus provides everything we need.*

OBJECTIVES

Kids will

✓ be grouped into "families" and walk together,

✓ participate in an interactive story of the feeding of the five thousand,

✓ make a stretchy fish to use in retelling the story to their families, and

✓ practice telling today's Bible story with a partner.

BIBLE BASIS   Read

 Mark 6:14-44; John 6:1-14

The feeding of the five thousand is certainly one of Jesus' most remarkable miracles; in fact, the feeding and the Resurrection are the only miracles reported in all four Gospels.

This was an emotional time for Jesus. He'd just gotten the news that John the Baptist had been beheaded at the whim of Herod's stepdaughter after she performed a dance that pleased Herod at his birthday party. Herod immediately regretted his offer to give her anything she desired, but to save face he ordered the beheading of the imprisoned John.

When John's disciples brought the tragic news to Jesus, he

You'll need...

☐ three to four 4-foot diameter circles made from twine or cotton cording (1 for every 3 or 4 kids)

☐ five 20-inch lengths of elastic or twine

☐ large package of fish-shaped crackers* poured into a paper grocery bag that is then stapled shut

☐ paper plates and napkins

☐ 2 large green party tablecloths

☐ masking tape

☐ envelope with this message inside: "John the Baptist is dead!"

☐ copies of the "Stretchy Fish" handout (p. 106)

☐ scissors

* Always check for allergies before serving snacks.

wanted time alone. Leaving from Capernaum, he and his disciples sailed across the northern tip of the Sea of Galilee toward a rural area near Bethsaida. However, the masses of people wanting to see Jesus anticipated his direction, so that when the boat pulled toward shore Jesus found not solitude but a huge crowd awaiting him. Scripture notes that there were 5,000 men. Adding women and children, the total number of people in the crowd had to have been at least 10,000! Rather than retreating from this daunting gathering, Jesus had compassion on the people; he healed their sick and taught them.

As evening drew near, Jesus asked his disciple Philip how the people could be fed. Philip pointed out that even if the disciples worked for months, they wouldn't be able to buy food for everyone. Only in John's Gospel does it tell that Andrew brought forward a young boy who wanted to offer his food of five small loaves and two fish. Bless Andrew not only for seeing the child, but also for seeing with eyes of faith what Jesus might do with such modest beginnings.

Jesus had the people sit in groups of fifty and a hundred, much as an army would be organized. Jesus took the bread and blessed it and then gave it to the disciples to distribute to the hungry people. Then he did the same with the fish. Afterward, the disciples picked up 12 baskets of leftovers. With this miracle, Jesus showed himself to be greater than Moses! The next day, Jesus explained that the bread he gave represented eternal life, but the people in the crowd of about 10,000 could only think about their full bellies. Right after the miraculous feeding, the people wanted to make Jesus king. To foil their plans, he slipped away and went off into the mountains by himself. The disciples took off in their boat again and the huge crowd dispersed.

 Deuteronomy 8:1–3

For Jewish people who were raised on stories of their ancestors, what did it mean that Jesus produced bread for the hungry? A great deal! For one thing, here was a prophet greater than Moses— the one they esteemed more than anyone. Moses only *told* of the manna that God would drop on the camp of the wandering Israelites. Jesus himself *produced* the bread to feed the masses and later went on to proclaim himself to be the bread of life.

This symbolism wouldn't have been missed by any of Jesus' followers. A prophet greater than Moses? This must be the Messiah. Let's make him king!

All Together Now

Jesus taught over and over that his was not the role of conquering king, but the role of suffering servant who would give his life for the ransom of many. It was a lesson even his own disciples couldn't accept or understand at this point. It brought such disappointment that in the end, it was easy to influence crowds—who were only seeing the short view—against him. They wanted full bellies, not full hearts. They wanted their hero to shove Herod and Rome aside, not to succumb to a criminal's death.

From this point on, the Sadducees, Pharisees, and teachers of the law would see Jesus as a much greater threat than they had before.

UNDERSTANDING YOUR KIDS

Would kids rather have a full belly or a contented heart? Kids live much more in the "now" than adults do, so a full belly will win almost every time.

However, we never know when the Holy Spirit will speak to the hearts of the children we teach. You'll find that kids who've been through grief and very difficult circumstances will often identify hunger for God's reassuring presence in their hearts at quite a young age.

Because you're teaching kids of mixed ages, some of them will receive this lesson at a deeper level than others. That's fine. As your more God-hungry kids interact with the lesson, they'll begin to open others' eyes.

Even if you're only planting the first seeds of the complex idea of the heart that's hungry for God, who knows when the Holy Spirit will bring it to mind? The next time the child eats fish crackers? goes fishing? goes on a picnic? feels heartache over a friend's betrayal?

How precious are those first seeds you plant! You're partnering with the Holy Spirit to help children understand Jesus in a new way and to change their hearts forever. As you have fun with the rowdy parts of this lesson, bear in mind that everything you do is leading toward making an eternal difference.

ATTENTION GRABBER

Hoop Family Dash

Greet kids warmly and ask about what's been going on in their lives this past week.

Say: **Today we're going to revisit one of Jesus' greatest miracles. It's such a great miracle that it's told four times in the Bible. You'll see in this amazing miracle how ★ *Jesus provides everything we need.***

Learning about such a miracle requires a little preparation. A *lot* of preparation, actually. I hope you're up for a workout! But don't worry—this isn't a go-it alone activity. Watch out, because I'm about to grab you into Hoop Families!

Use twine hoops to encircle three to four children each, depending on the size of your group. Aim for a mix of younger and older children in each family.

Say: **OK, families, here comes the big connection.**

Attach an elastic cord to each hoop circle, and then attach the loose ends of the elastic cords to the end of another cord. This last cord acts as your "lead rope."

Pull on your lead rope gently to lead the Hoop Families around the room. This will lead to lots of giggling as the children learn how to move together inside their hoop rings. As you move along, say: **Wherever Jesus traveled in Galilee, he taught about the kingdom of God, not about things a regular teacher might teach about. He taught about a loving God who wanted to forgive people and give them new life. And Jesus also healed the sick. So when word came that Jesus was in the neighborhood, everyone hurried to bring their sick friends and relatives to him.**

"Hurry" your Hoop Families into a brisk walk. Take them around the room, into the hallway, or even outside if it's a nice day. Make sure your Families end up panting a bit. Then release the elastic cords.

Say: **Jesus didn't usually stay in one place for long, so the crowds felt that if they hurried to be the first to see Jesus, they'd win the big prize of getting close to him and having their relatives healed.**

Hold up the bag with the fish crackers.

Say: **Here's the big prize. Taking care that no one in your family falls down or gets hurt, let's see which family can get to the prize first!**

All Together Now

Toss the bag of treats as far from the Families as possible. Cheer on the Families as they try to get to the prize first.

Say to the winning Family as you take the bag of treats: **Good job! I'll hold on to that for you until we get to our story area.**

Say: **Of course, when the families all got to Jesus, they made a great circle around him so they could get close to hear him and maybe even touch him. Families, make a big circle around me and then walk quickly around me, making sure to keep pace with everyone else in your family.**

Let the families keep walking quickly until you have a hilarious group of tired, out-of-sync Families.

Say: **Families, it looks like you're ready for a rest! When I say** three**, drop to the floor together. Ready? One, two,** three**! Now take some nice deep breaths.**

Because you did such a good job working together, you can put your hoops around me and lead me to the story area. Gently, please. Remember, I'm holding the treats!

BIBLE EXPLORATION
....

Jesus and the Humongous Picnic (Mark 6:14-44; John 6:1-14)

Say: **Take off your shoes and place them against that wall.** Indicate a wall. **Good. Now help me spread out and tape down these green tablecloths. I'll tell you what they represent a little bit later.** Spread out the tablecloths for maximum area coverage and tape them at the corners and between the two cloths. **Excellent. Now we're ready to go.**

You may be surprised to learn that this great miracle began with Jesus getting some really bad news. I have an envelope with the bad news in it right here. Who would like to open it?

You may want to let a younger child open the envelope and ask an older child to help read the note inside.

The note reads, *John the Baptist is dead!*

Say: **That was terrible news for Jesus! John the Baptist and Jesus were cousins. John the Baptist was the one who baptized Jesus at the beginning of Jesus' ministry. And John the Baptist had been in prison for a long time. King Herod had John the Baptist killed.** Ask kids to show you what they look like when they get really bad news.

When John's disciples came to Jesus with the sad news, Jesus decided to take his disciples in a fishing boat and sail to a place where they could be alone for a while. Jesus wanted to spend time praying to God. Ask kids to show you what they look like when they pray.

But the crowds of people who wanted to see Jesus watched to see which way his boat sailed and they took their families and started running along the shoreline as fast as they could. Ask kids to show you what they look like when they run.

When Jesus and his disciples pulled into shore, they didn't find the nice, quiet place they were hoping for. Instead, they found a huge crowd of thousands of people waiting for them.

Ask:

• What could Jesus have done when he saw the crowds waiting on the shore?

Say: He could've had the disciples sail away to a different place, or he could've pulled into shore and faced the thousands of people who'd come to see him. The Bible says that Jesus had compassion for the crowds, because they were like sheep without a shepherd.

Ask:

• What do you think "sheep without a shepherd" means?

Say: Jesus and his disciples pulled their boat up to the shore to meet the crowds. Jesus took time to teach the people and to heal the sick who were there. It wasn't the day of rest and prayer he imagined, but he loved people too much to brush them aside.

As the sun began to sink in the sky, the disciples grew nervous. There was no way to feed the huge crowd. The disciples asked Jesus what to do. Ask kids to show you what they look like when they don't know what to do.

Then the disciple Andrew brought forward a little boy who was willing to share his food of five small loaves of bread and two fishes. Jesus had the disciples tell the people to sit down on the green grass, kind of like you're sitting on these green tablecloths. Then he took the little boy's loaves, gave thanks to God for them, and broke the bread and had the disciples distribute it to the groups sitting on the grass. Then he did the same with the fish. From that one little meal, that whole crowd of about 10,000 people ate all they wanted. Ask kids to show you what they look like when they're full.

Open the stapled grocery bag of fish crackers and toss a fish cracker in the air for each child to catch. Then serve a paper plate

All Together Now

of fish to each child. Give kids napkins to wipe their hands when finished.

Say: **That was one humongous picnic! After everyone finished eating, the disciples went around and picked up 12 baskets of leftovers. All from one little boy's meal!**

Seeing Jesus' great miracle, some of the people began to make plans to take Jesus and make him king by force. But instead of staying with the crowd, Jesus went off to a mountaintop to be by himself.

Ask:

• **Why did people follow Jesus even when he wanted to be alone?**

• **What do you think of what Jesus did?**

Say: **Let's make something to remind us that ★ *Jesus provides everything we need.***

Have kids put on their shoes.

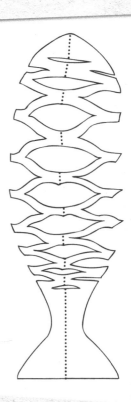

Prep Box

Set out scissors and copies of the "Stretchy Fish" handout. Have a stretchy fish prepared so kids can see a sample of what they'll be making.

LIFE APPLICATION

Stretchy Fish

Lead the kids to the craft table where you've set out the supplies.

Say: **Today we're going to make a really cool fish you can use to help you retell our Bible story to your families. It's simple but tricky at the same time. Look what happens when you follow the cutting directions exactly.**

Display the stretchy fish you folded and cut before class. Be prepared for oohs and ahs!

Say: **Listen carefully as I guide you through the process of making the fish.**

✓ Fold your handout in half on the dotted line. Crease your fold nicely.

✓ Cut the outline of the fish from A to B.

✓ Cut carefully on the black lines, some from the center and some from the outside.

✓ When you've finished cutting, gently pull your fish at both ends and watch it stretch!

If kids make a wrong cut, give them another copy of the handout and a bit of assistance getting started.

Teacher Tip

Have older kids seated next to younger kids to keep an eye on the younger ones' cutting. It's very simple but requires a bit of concentration.

Stretchy Fish

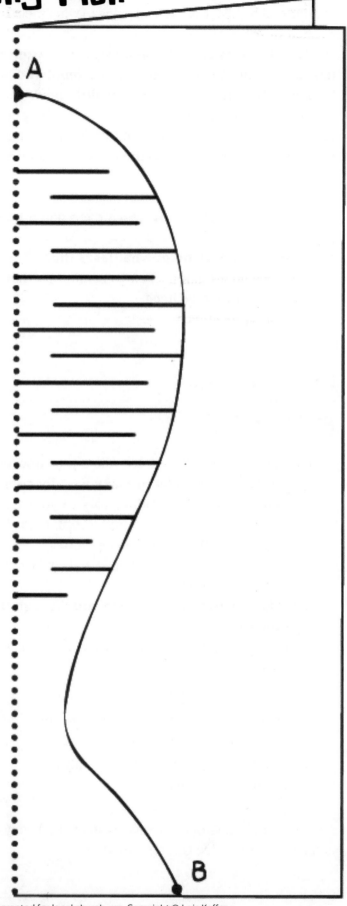

When kids are done, say: **Check this out! We have a whole bunch of fish right here before our very eyes. Look at how the fish stretches, like the way Jesus' miracle stretched two fish to be enough for thousands of people.**

COMMITMENT

Pair Story Telling

Have kids form pairs and take turns telling each other about the feeding of the five thousand using their stretchy fish. If a partner gets stuck, the other partner can offer prompts.

After giving the kids a few minutes to practice their stories, ask:

• **What are the most important parts you'll remember to include in your story?**

• **What kinds of questions will you ask your families after you tell the story?**

Say: **When you share God's Word each week, you're doing an important job for Jesus. The very last command Jesus gave his disciples before he rose into heaven was, "Go into all the earth and preach the gospel." When you share God's Word at home, you're helping tell the good news about Jesus. Great job!**

CLOSING

Say: **Let's gather for prayer.**

Dear Jesus, thank you for teaching us that you ★ *provide everything we need* and take away the hunger inside our hearts. We thank and praise you for being such an amazing Savior. Amen.

Jesus Breaks Down Walls

You'll need...

- ☐ about 48 brown paper lunch bags (to build a bigger wall, gather large, grocery-size paper bags—many grocery stores, hardware stores, and office supply store still use the larger paper bags)
- ☐ masking tape
- ☐ copies of the "Sychar Scribbler" handout (p. 117)
- ☐ pencils
- ☐ 2 Bibles

LESSON AIM

To help kids learn how ★ *Jesus helps people be friends.*

OBJECTIVES

Kids will

- ✓ build a wall of lunch-bag bricks and then take turns trying to keep it up and knock it down,
- ✓ use their lunch-bag brick to participate in an interactive story of Jesus and the woman at the well,
- ✓ write articles for *The Sychar Scribbler* newspaper, and
- ✓ pray for God to help them help people be friends the way Jesus did.

BIBLE BASIS

 John 4:1-42

Normally when Jews of Jesus' time traveled between Judea and Galilee, they skirted away from Samaria, stretching a trip of about two and a half days into one almost twice as long. Animosities between Jews and Samaritans that had begun hundreds of years before were so tense that the two groups wanted as little as possible to do with each other. These animosities were the outcome of the fall of the northern kingdom of Israel to Assyria. The Jews in the Samaritan region freely intermarried with the Assyrians and thus picked up many foreign customs. But the Jews that remained in Judea and those carried off to Babylon were careful to marry only Jews. When the Judean Jews returned to rebuild the walls of Jerusalem and the Temple, they were still of "pure" Jewish blood, while the Samaritan blood was so "mixed" it was thought they hardly had any right to call themselves Jews at all.

Therefore, Jews who wanted to remain ritually clean avoided Samaria, taking a much longer route. On this particular occasion, Jesus deviated from this custom. He'd presented himself first to the Jews and now had no problem sharing his message in that somewhat hostile area. You might say he kicked down the walls of frigid cultural relations between the two communities of people.

But this is just the first wall Jesus would break down in this remarkable moment, recorded only by John.

Jesus and his disciples came to Jacob's well outside the town of Sychar. While the disciples went into town to get something to eat, Jesus chose to rest by the well. Soon a woman came to get water. She came alone and in the heat of the day rather than with a group of women in the cool of the morning or the evening. This solo trip signaled that the woman was likely some kind of outcast. Jesus broke two more protocols by asking the woman for something to drink: (1) Jews did not speak to Samaritans, and (2) men did not speak to women in public. When the disciples returned they were shocked by their rabbi's behavior but didn't dare ask him about it.

Jesus spoke prophetically to the woman about her life: She'd had five husbands and the man she was currently living with was not her husband. That got her attention! Caught off-guard by Jesus' bold statements about living water and eternal life, she changed the subject to something she could understand—why the Jews worshipped in Jerusalem and the Samaritans on Mount Gerizim. But Jesus wasn't about to let up on her. He said that soon it wouldn't matter *where* people worship, because true worshippers would worship God in spirit and in truth. This must've been a spiritually perceptive woman, because she began to inch toward the truth. "I know the Messiah is coming...he will explain everything to us."

Then Jesus boldly declared himself: "I Am the Messiah."

With that, the woman took off running to the village to encourage others to come hear this rabbi who told her all about herself. "Could he be the Messiah?" she asked. A crowd followed her back to the well and Jesus, and then they begged Jesus to stay in their town. Jesus stayed there for two days. And many of them believed in Jesus.

Suppose Jesus had chosen to step around Samaria? Are there areas you tend to "step around"? Let God open your mind to

All Together Now

breaking down walls in your life as you prepare to teach about this remarkable Jesus to your children.

 Psalm 22:22-28

The Samaritan woman at the well personified a stunning number of aspects of Psalm 22. She proclaimed Jesus to her neighbors and praised him among the assembled people. Jesus didn't ignore her or belittle her or turn his back on her. And though Samaria hardly represented the promise that "the whole earth" would acknowledge the Lord (Psalm 22:27), it was a beginning. When Jesus spoke to his disciples in Acts 1:8 just before rising into the clouds, he said, "You will receive power when the Holy Spirit comes upon you. And you will be my witnesses, telling people about me everywhere—in Jerusalem, throughout Judea, in *Samaria,* and to the ends of the earth" (emphasis added). While others might hesitate to go into Samaria, Jesus himself had already started a group of believers there. Jesus calls us to go to our own "Samarias" and to follow his example. ★ *Jesus helps people be friends.*

UNDERSTANDING YOUR KIDS

I've observed that whether there are "in" and "out" groups within a children's ministry largely depends on parents and teachers keeping a diligent eye out and stopping cliques before they have a chance to solidly form, as well as on teachers constantly mixing children in pairs and group activities. Kids form groups with those who are familiar to them. So make everyone familiar, and you're likely to be successful in maintaining an open, friendly atmosphere in your ministry. It takes work for kids to be paired with someone new. They may grumble in the beginning, but soon they'll get used to the pattern of being paired and grouped and it won't be strange at all.

In today's Bible passage, Jesus chose someone who at first might not have seemed a likely candidate for all the tremendous teaching he was about to give her. She was obviously an outcast without a great moral record, but look at how she stepped up to the plate and not only received everything Jesus had to say, but also turned into an ardent witness as well.

The truth is, you may have qualms about some kids who drop into your ministry, whether you want to admit it or not. Should you get a child who looks more like a misplaced stray than one who'll stick around, remember what Jesus did.

ATTENTION GRABBER

Build a Brick, Build a Wall

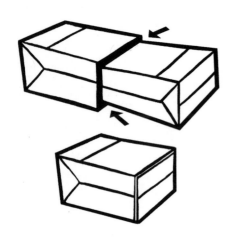

Greet kids warmly and engage them in conversation about what's been happening in their lives.

Say: **OK, everybody, I've got a major building project for us today and we've only got a few minutes to complete it. Let's get started!**

Pick up two flattened lunch bags.

Say: **These are our basic materials. Watch how quickly they'll help us get the job done.**

Hand one bag to a younger child with instructions to open it. Open the remaining bag yourself. Tell the younger child: **Hold the mouth of your bag wide open while I pinch the mouth of my bag a bit, so it's just small enough to fit inside yours.**

Once your bag is inside the other, let it go back to full size and push it all the way to the back of the child's bag, forming a sturdy, two-bag brick. Hold up the brick and show it to the rest of the kids.

Say: **Now it's your turn to be brick makers. Find a partner who's older or younger than you. To begin, each pair can take six bags and make three bricks with them, just like we did. Let's build some bricks!**

Have pairs take their bags and spread out all over the room. You and an assistant can move about among the pairs to provide assistance as needed. Keep on building bricks until pairs have used up all the bags.

Say: **What a bunch of beautiful bricks! You might be wondering what we're going to do with them. Never fear—I have a plan. To begin, gently bring your bricks over here by me.** Stand near the center of the room.

Have kids count the number of bricks they've made to determine what size wall they'll build. For instance, if your kids have made 24 bricks, plan to build a wall that's four bricks across and six bricks tall. Whatever your dimensions, you'll want a wall that's slightly taller than it is wide.

Have about half the pairs of kids lay the first row of the wall. Then have the rest of the pairs lay the second row. Alternate groups of kids until the wall is complete, providing steadying hands as the wall grows.

Say: **Now that's what I call a good-looking wall!**

This wall is kind of like the walls we build in our hearts. Do you know we build walls in our hearts? Oh, we do! For

instance, this first row might be a wall that keeps out people who look a little different than we're used to. The second row might be a wall that keeps out people who've made us angry or upset. We might not feel like being around them anymore. Let's see—the third row could keep out people who are outside our normal group of friends. We're not mad at them, they haven't hurt us, it's just that we're not used to hanging out with them, so we don't. We're probably not even aware that there's any barrier dividing us.

Ask kids to think about things that divide them from other people.

Say: **Because we often don't even notice these walls in our hearts, they can be pretty difficult to knock down. The longer they're there, the more they want to stay in place.**

Now, you're looking at this wall and thinking it'd be pretty easy to knock down, aren't you? Well, I don't think it'll be easy at all.

Have kids get back into their groups, and then move the groups to opposite sides of the wall. Point to one group, and say: **You'll be the "Bashers." You'll throw the bricks I give you at the wall to try to knock it down.** Turn to the other group. **You'll be the "Balancers." You'll support the wall with your bodies and hands, any way you can to keep it from toppling over.**

Make a masking tape line on the floor a few feet back from the wall for the Bashers to stand behind. Then "arm" the Bashers with one brick per child from the top row of the wall.

Say: **Bashers, you need to stand behind this line when you throw bricks at the wall. Everyone in your group gets two tosses. Are you ready? Let's go!**

It's likely that the Balancers will be able to keep most of the wall intact.

Say: **OK, let's firm up the wall and then have the Bashers and Balancers trade roles.**

Play the game again with the groups in opposite roles. Then gather everyone for discussion.

Say: **In our Bible passage today, Jesus will break down a lot of walls—not by throwing bricks at them, but by the way he treats people. After you hear this passage, I'm going to ask you about the ways you heard ★** *Jesus helping people be friends.*

....

Jesus Breaks Down Walls (John 4:1-42)

Say: **You're going to be very busy moving bricks around to help me tell our Bible story, so please line up until I point at you to give you a job. Once you've completed your job, please return to the line again. There *will* be a point when you'll get to sit down, I promise. But not yet!**

Say: **The Jews and the Samaritans were *not* friends. In fact, they hadn't been friends for hundreds of years.** Have each child get a brick and together build a wall with all the bricks. **So if a group of Jews in Jerusalem wanted to travel to Galilee, they usually went out of their way to stay out of Samaria.** Have kids split up, with half of them on the Jewish side and half on the Samaritan side of the wall. **Traveling to Galilee this way took twice as long.**

Say: **On this particular day, Jesus told his disciples that he needed to go through Samaria. Jesus didn't explain why, and the disciples didn't ask.** Have half of the Jewish side move to the Samaritan side. **The disciples may've been nervous, because the Jews and the Samaritans hated each other, and here they were, walking right through Samaria. About noon they came to an old well outside the village of Sychar. All of you can work together to take the bricks and build a round well. Jesus was tired and decided to sit down and rest. I'm going to sit down and watch you build the well.** Allow time. You may need to provide a little technical assistance as the kids attempt to build a round well from rectangular bricks.

After the well is built, say: **While the disciples went to find something to eat, Jesus stayed by the well to rest.** Have everyone move to a distant corner of the room. **Pretty soon a woman came to the well all by herself.** Have an older girl return to the well. **Jesus knew it was strange for a woman to come by herself to the well in the heat of the day. Normally women came with friends when it was cool outside in the evening or early morning. But this woman came alone when it was very hot.**

Jesus knew she didn't have any friends.

Jesus asked the woman for a drink of water. She almost jumped in surprise.

Let's read in the Bible to see what happened next.

Keep a Bible yourself and give the girl a Bible opened to John 4.

All Together Now

Have the girl read the woman's speaking parts while you read Jesus' speaking parts, starting in verse 9 and ending in verse 26.

Say: **Everything Jesus said rang true in the woman's heart. He was the Messiah? She had to go tell the people in her town! She ran to Sychar and shouted to everyone, "Come and see a man who told me everything I ever did! Could he possibly be the Messiah?"**

Have the older girl run to the kids standing in the corner and repeat the lines: *Come and see a man who told me everything I ever did! Could he possibly be the Messiah?*

Say: **An entire crowd of people came back to the well.** Motion for all the kids to join you by the well again. **They listened to Jesus teach and then they begged him to stay in their village. And many people in the village of Sychar believed Jesus truly was the Messiah.**

Say: **What a great job you all did helping tell this story. Give yourselves a big stomping, clapping cheer! Woo-hoo!**

Ask:

• **What was the most surprising way Jesus broke down walls between people?**

• **What kind of walls do you have between yourself and others?**

• **How might Jesus help you break down those walls?**

LIFE APPLICATION
. . . .

The Sychar Scribbler

Say: **Jesus' talk with the woman at the well and his two-day stay in Sychar to teach the people there must've been quite an earth-shaking event for folks from that village. Let's suppose they had a little village newspaper that came out once a week. Perhaps it was called *The Sychar Scribbler.***

There would've been a lot of things to write about the week Jesus came to town! Guess what? You're all officially reporters for *The Sychar Scribbler* as of this very moment. You'll work together in groups of three. To build your group, please find three people of different ages.

Share your ideas for a news report about what happened when Jesus came to Sychar. You might choose to do a first-person report from the woman at the well or from someone in town who ran to the well to see what was going on.

Or you might choose to write it as a regular news report. Maybe you'll want to make your news report in comic-strip form. What you write and how you write it is all up to you. I'm going to give you plenty of time so you can write your report on each group member's paper. I'll even come around and give you a hand!

Don't try to make your news report look absolutely perfect, because you only have time to do a rough draft.

Once I hand out your newspapers and pencils, take your writing group to any part of the room and get to work. Here we go!

You may need to help kids form groups. It's fine to have a group of four or a group of two if that works best for your kids. Move to each group quickly to help them get started. An extra assistant in your room is great for this activity.

Give your young reporters as much time as possible to work on their newspaper reports. Five minutes before the end of class, bring everyone together. Have kids from each group who didn't do the main part of the writing or drawing stand and read the reports. Give a hearty round of applause for each report.

COMMITMENT
. . . .

Wall Breakers

Say: **Whew! We've done a lot today!**
Ask:
• **What did you learn today?**
• **What's one way you'll break down a wall that separates you from someone this week?**

You have a fun newspaper to share with your family that features your very own story about what happened when Jesus met the woman at the well. But that's not all you're going to take home! You each get to take a brick, too, so you can talk about how ★ *Jesus helps people be friends.*

Plan to recycle leftover lunch bags.

All Together Now

The Sychar Scribbler

Sychar Meets the Messiah!

WANT ADS

Wanted:
Plump sheep for cheap.

Bethany's Bakery
You knead our bread!

Caleb's Carpentry
Doors and door frames.
We've got you pegged!

Tovar's Tannery
Tanning your hides for
more than 20 years.

Miriam's Mourners
We wail till the world
wails with us.

Sheep Shearing
Sharpest knives. We'll
fleece you good!

Published in *All Together Now, Volume 2* by Group Publishing, Inc., 1515 Cascade Ave., Loveland, CO 80538.

....

How Shall We Pray

Ask:

•**What shall we pray about today? I'd like your ideas.**

Encourage the children to pray about the concerns they raise. Close by asking God to help everyone follow the example of ★*Jesus helping people be friends.*

All Together Now

Through the Roof!

You'll need...

- ☐ masking tape
- ☐ 3 large cardboard boxes with the sides cut open to create large, flat pieces of cardboard
- ☐ brightly colored scarf
- ☐ Bible
- ☐ sturdy blanket
- ☐ whiteboard and marker
- ☐ copies of the "Good Friend" handout (p. 128)
- ☐ pencils or fine-tipped markers

LESSON AIM

To help kids see that ★ *friends can help each other follow Jesus.*

OBJECTIVES

Kids will

- ✓ participate in "drag races" with cut-open cardboard boxes,
- ✓ act out parts in an interactive telling of the paralyzed man lowered through the roof,
- ✓ brainstorm what makes a good friend and write affirmations on each other's "Good Friend" handouts, and
- ✓ discover ways they can be better friends.

BIBLE BASIS

 Mark 2:1-12

I remember a less-than-respectful saying that went around the basketball community a few years back. It happened when an offensive player slam-dunked the ball practically in the face of the ineffective defender, and it went something like, "In-your-face disgrace, man!"

Not good sportsmanship, but the exchange has a certain way of capturing the confrontation between Jesus and the out-to-get-him teachers of religious law in this Bible account.

The Old Testament makes no mention of these "teachers of religious law" who so often appeared to heckle Jesus. So who were they? In Old Testament times they were originally simple scribes who made copies of the Scriptures and did secretarial duties for the priests. While the Jews were in exile, though, their role expanded. With no Temple and the order of priests scattered hither and yon, the scribes were sometimes the closest a Jewish community had to an expert in the law. More than copiers of Scripture, they became teachers and interpreters of it. While the priests remained close to Jerusalem to carry out the duties in the Temple in their turn, the teachers of the law might rove throughout the land with some freedom and expect the respect of the people.

These teachers of the law decided to take on Jesus in Capernaum, his home base—mistake number one. They cared nothing for Jesus' teachings and healings that thrilled and astonished others—mistake number two. They were simply there to look down their noses at this upstart rabbi and catch him doing something wrong; their minds and hearts were completely closed to the grace of God that surrounded them—mistake number three.

It may be hard for us to imagine people with such an attitude toward Jesus: How could the teachers of the law listen to Jesus' remarkable message and watch him heal suffering people with his compassionate hands and fail to be moved?

Can the answer be as simple as that they desired power? Before the coming of John the Baptist and Jesus, Israel had been without a prophet for hundreds of years. Leading the people had long since become less a matter of devotion to God and more a civic matter. These teachers of the law often were those born into the "right" families. They studied for years and years to attain distinction. Most of them could recite entire sections of the Old Testament from memory. Now that they'd finally attained the revered status they sought, who should come along but some no-name peasant from an agricultural village with no great cultural or learning center tied to it at all.

Their status had been usurped—suddenly, inexplicably, and soon it was their fear, permanently. So they were there to outplay Jesus even when he was surrounded by his most enthusiastic supporters. They had far more interest in defending their pride and regaining their place of power and respect than in opening their minds to any new truth God might be revealing through this rabbi from Galilee, of all places. How sad to be so close to the Son of God and so immune to his glory!

A certain paralyzed man had four great friends who carried

All Together Now

him to the house where Jesus was teaching and healing. The house was packed and the crowds spilled into the street. The chances of getting their friend in to see Jesus were nonexistent. But these friends didn't give up easily. Up the side stairs they lugged him, and out onto the roof. Estimating where Jesus must be teaching below, they began digging through the branches and mud of the roof. I imagine the debris falling on the solemn faces of Jesus' critics. Soon the men had a hole large enough to accommodate their paralyzed friend on his mat, so through the hole he went.

Jesus wasn't annoyed by the falling roof, but amazed by the faith of the five friends. So he looked at the paralyzed man and said, "My child, your sins are forgiven." We have no way of knowing, but it's possible that Jesus made this word choice to annoy his critics, who immediately began to think to themselves, *This is blasphemy! Only God can forgive sins!*

Jesus' response is so beautiful:

Jesus knew immediately what they were thinking, so he asked them, "Why do you question this in your hearts? Is it easier to say to the paralyzed man 'Your sins are forgiven,' or 'Stand up, pick up your mat, and walk'? So I will prove to you that the Son of Man has the authority on Earth to forgive sins.' " Then Jesus turned to the paralyzed man and said, "Stand up, pick up your mat, and go home!" (Mark 2:8-12)

And all who believed in Jesus pumped their fists and shouted, "YES!"

 Malachi 2:1-9; 3:1

This passage describes how far the priestly line of Israel had fallen from God's original design. Rather than leading the people toward God and his holiness, they had fallen into secularism and greed. Theirs was no longer a faithful interpretation of the law, but one that saw to their own benefit, in stark contrast to the original descendents of Levi, on whom the priesthood was based.

What more perfect language could describe the unexpected coming of Jesus than this: " 'Then the Lord you are seeking will suddenly come to his Temple. The messenger of the covenant, whom you look for so eagerly, is surely coming,' says the Lord of Heaven's Armies" (Malachi 3:1).

The slackers were caught slacking. The holier-than-thous suddenly didn't look so holy. Religious leaders who'd lost their passion for God suddenly looked pale in comparison with the winsome ways of Jesus of Nazareth. Jesus' miracles pulsed with the mystery of the living God. He healed broken bodies, turned lives inside out, and ignited a new passion for God in Israel—but all the teachers of the law could do was nitpick, unmoved and uncaring.

Suddenly the Lord had come to his temple. A new living covenant had begun to overshadow the old. Blessed were those who saw and believed. To be pitied were those who couldn't.

UNDERSTANDING YOUR KIDS

This is one of the most touching stories of friendship in all of Scripture. For the paralyzed man and his entourage were not only friends, they were also people bound by unbreakable faith. Their goal: to get the paralyzed friend to see Jesus. The problem: There was no way to get through the crowd and into the house. The solution: Climb to the roof, dig through it, and lower the paralyzed man through. Sure, I'd have thought of that, wouldn't you?

Your kids can't choose how their friends will behave, but they can choose what kind of friends *they* will be. In the face of overwhelming discouragement, will they be friends who stick on the side of faith?

There's no Bible account better than this one to challenge your kids to be that kind of friend, to be Jesus-followers with a whatever-it-takes attitude. You surely don't hope that they'll be digging holes in roofs next week! But they might be there for a friend who's taking excessive teasing, offer encouragement to someone who's down, or even pray with a fellow Christian who's up against a problem.

Use this lesson to help your kids find practical ways to follow Jesus in their friendships.

All Together Now

ATTENTION GRABBER

. . . .

Cardboard Drag Relays

Greet kids warmly as they arrive.

Form a circle and say: **If your family sometimes likes to watch car races, raise your hand. You probably know that there are lots of different kinds of sports racing on TV. One that's really different from the rest is called drag racing.**

If you have a child who's familiar with drag racing, let him or her explain. Otherwise, continue with your own explanation.

Say: **Drag racing has all different kinds of funny-looking cars and very short races. Two cars race against each other to see which can go a quarter mile the fastest. Vroom-vroom and it's over. Like other kinds of car racing, it's quite dangerous because the cars are superpowerful and have to be controlled to make high-speed takeoffs and travel in a straight line. Only highly trained drivers and crews can perform these races on special tracks with emergency personnel standing by.**

It's something that no one must ever try off a racetrack or without years and years of specialized training. Do you hear me loud and clear? The answer to that is "Loud and clear!" with a big salute. Do you hear me loud and clear?

Lead kids in responding with "Loud and clear!" with a big salute.

That's what I like to hear!

The good news is that today I have some safe drag relay races set up right here that will be a ton of fun! It doesn't matter at all who finishes first; the goal is for all of us to finish without falling off our cardboard cars.

Here's how the relay works. Pair up with a relay partner who is as close to your own size as possible. Let's do that right now. Pause as kids pair up.

Now because this is a *drag* relay, you'll begin with one person sitting on the cardboard and the other person dragging the Rider to the opposite wall. When the Dragger touches the opposite wall, you switch roles, so the Dragger becomes the Rider and the Rider starts dragging. When you get back to the starting line, tag the next team in line to go. Remember: This isn't a race. Your job is to keep your Rider safe and still sitting on the cardboard car by the time you

Prep Box

You'll need an open area for this relay activity, so clear obstacles from the middle of your teaching area. Lay a masking-tape line as far as you can from an open wall. Place three cut-open cardboard boxes behind the masking-tape line.

Teacher Tip

You may need to reshuffle pairs a bit to help each person find a partner near his or her own size. Feel free to put an adult assistant in the mix!

return. **If your Rider falls off, you start over. Let's see how well our whole class can finish this drag relay.**

Line up pairs as equally as possible behind your three cardboard "cars." If you have a short line, one pair from another line may volunteer to go twice. Point out to the Draggers that it's easy to pull the flattened cardboard box by one of the cut-apart panels.

Wave a bright scarf to start the relay. Encourage the waiting kids to clap and cheer loudly for the kids on the course. If a child topples off the cardboard, have that pair go back to the starting line or the wall to begin again.

When everyone's done, gather the cardboard and say: **You may wonder what this has to do with today's Bible's story about how ★ *friends can help each other follow Jesus*. I'm going to satisfy your curiosity, but I'll need lots of help from you to tell the story. Let's get started!**

BIBLE EXPLORATION

Through the Roof (Mark 2:1-12)

Say: **After having been away for a while, Jesus once again returned to his home base, the town of Capernaum. People were eager to hear him teach, so they hurried to the house where Jesus was staying.**

Ask a willing child to read aloud Mark 2:1-3.

I need two people to stand and be the door of the home where Jesus is teaching. I need five people to step aside for another task. Everyone else crowd around the door of the home where Jesus is teaching. (If you have fewer kids, reduce these numbers to fit your group.)

Now inside the house, probably in the front row, we have some teachers of religious law. These men don't like Jesus and are hoping to catch him make some little mistake. So everyone do this with me: these men are stroking their beards (pretend to stroke your beard) **and looking down their long noses** (pretend to look haughtily down your long nose)**, hoping to show that they're smarter than Jesus. Now we're all set up for the next surprising thing to happen.**

Call up the five kids you set apart earlier. Whip out a sturdy blanket, and instruct the smallest of the five to lie down in its center. Instruct the other four to pick of the corners of the blanket and slide their friend to the door of the house where Jesus is

All Together Now

teaching. Avoid having kids actually carry the child to avoid any injuries.

Say: **Here come four friends with a fifth friend who's paralyzed on his bed. All five of them believe that if the paralyzed man can get to see Jesus, Jesus will heal him. But they're running into a problem.**

Ask:

• **Describe what kind of problem you think they're facing.**

Say: **The house where Jesus is teaching is full. So full that people are spilling out into the street. Everyone is so excited to see Jesus that they're not about to make room for these four men to carry their paralyzed friend into the house to see Jesus. Hmm.**

Ask:

• **What options do you see in this situation?**

Ask kids who already know the story not to share "spoilers." Let the Carriers stand still with the Paralyzed Man on the floor as this discussion takes place.

Say: **One option might have been to give up and go home. After all, they'd done their best, hadn't they, carrying their friend all the way to this house where Jesus was teaching? Or what if they just left their friend outside the house? Jesus would eventually leave. He might stay overnight or maybe even two nights, but eventually he'd leave and if the paralyzed man was lucky, Jesus might see him when he left the house.**

Ask:

• **Tell why you think that's a good idea or a bad idea.**

• **Describe any other ideas you have.**

Say: **Well, let me tell you, these friends had real faith muscles.** (To the Carriers) **Show us the faith muscles you have there.** After their demonstration of muscles, say: **Of course, faith muscles don't really show that way, but you get the idea. They were going to get their paralyzed friend in to see Jesus no matter what it took!**

Have a willing child read aloud Mark 2:4.

Say: **Here's a cool thing about houses in Jesus' time: The roofs were built to be flat for a deck so people could go up on the roof and enjoy the cool of the evening in a hot climate. On one side of the house there were stairs that led up to the roof. So the four friends picked up the paralyzed friend and carried him to the stairs.**

Eight of you who were the door and the crowd, please

lie down and make yourselves evenly spaced to represent the stairs. Our brave friends will carry the paralyzed man up your stairs so they'll end up on the roof.

Once the Carriers and Paralyzed Man have negotiated the human staircase, say: **Check it out! You've made it to the roof of the house where Jesus is teaching. How about applause! Now, everyone but the Carriers and Paralyzed Man please form the outline of the roof.** Help kids form a square roof outline.

Once they made it to the rooftop, the friends had to guess where Jesus might be in the room below. They made their best guess and started digging with their hands. Carriers, down on your knees and start digging!

In Jesus' time, roofs were made of tree branches woven together and then filled in with clay made from mud. Not too hard to take apart, and not too hard to repair again. Everyone forming the outline of the roof, imagine you are the stuck-up teachers of religious law and all of a sudden debris from the roof starts falling in your face, on your beard, and all over your robes. Show us how annoyed you'd look as you brushed it off.

Pause as kids looked annoyed and brush themselves off.

Say: **Ooh—you're looking pretty annoyed! I think I'd want to stay away from you for a while!**

Finally the friends had made a hole that was big enough to fit their friend through. Everyone who's forming the roof, lie on the floor and crowd around so all we have is a hole of just the right size.

Carriers, slide your paralyzed friend into the hole.

Have a willing child read aloud Mark 2:5.

Right away the paralyzed man could feel strength pouring into his arms and legs that had been lifeless and limp for so long.

But Jesus' words got the teachers of religious law hopping mad. *Only God can forgive sins,* they thought. *If Jesus is making himself equal with God, this is a terrible sin!*

The Bible says that Jesus immediately knew what they were thinking.

Have a willing child read aloud Mark 2:8-12.

Signal your Paralyzed Man to stand and pick up his blanket.

Say: **When everyone saw the paralyzed man walking, they praised God and said, "We've never seen anything like this before!"**

All Together Now

The teachers of religious law had nothing to say in the face of Jesus' power. And as for the paralyzed man and his four faithful friends, well, you can imagine how much they rejoiced and thanked Jesus together!

Let's all join them in praising and thanking Jesus together!

Lead your kids in movements of joy and thanksgiving.

Say: **I can hardly imagine better friends than the paralyzed man's friends. There are many ways of being good friends. One of the best things about friendship is that ★*friends can help each other follow Jesus.* What that means is that you can help your friends follow Jesus.**

LIFE APPLICATION

Good Friend Affirmations

Go to a whiteboard and marker.

Say: **Let's think for a minute about what you look for in a good friend. Let's start with this: I look for a friend who is... and you finish the sentence as many different ways as you can. I'll jot down your ideas here.**

Keep brainstorming until you have at least one response from each child, but get even more than that if you can.

Say: **Now here's a fun twist. Look at all these ideas, but change the sentence to: I want to be a friend who is... Hmm. Wow—that becomes a challenge, doesn't it!**

I thought it might be encouraging to see how well your friends here think you're doing at being a friend.

Give each child a "Good Friend" handout and a pencil or fine-tipped marker. Have kids write their names on the blank line. Then begin passing the papers around so each child in the class has an opportunity to write an affirmation on every other child's paper. After kids have written their affirmations, have them sign their initials. Encourage kids to look at your whiteboard if they need ideas. Be on hand to help younger kids who are not yet confident writers, and let them draw illustrations if they'd rather.

When kids' handouts are returned to them, watch their smiles as they read what others have written about them!

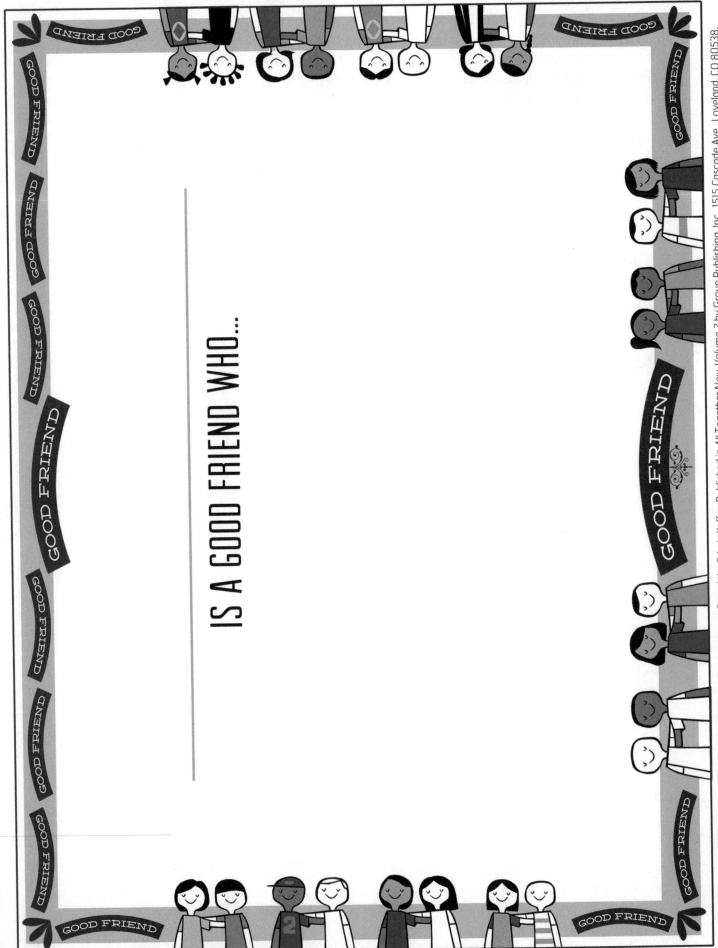

IS A GOOD FRIEND WHO...

COMMITMENT

Better Friend Challenge

Ask:

• **How did seeing affirmations from your friends encourage you?**

• **The four friends in the Bible story had one goal. What surprised you about that goal?**

• **What might that goal look like in today's world?**

• **How can you help your friends follow Jesus?**

Have kids find their partners from the drag relays and plan three ways they'll be good friends this week.

CLOSING

Friend Prayers

To close, have kids remain in pairs. Have children each pray for their partners to find ways to be a good friend this week.

Remind kids to take their good friend affirmations when they leave.

Who's the Greatest?

You'll need...

- ☐ a copy of the "Cast of the Castle" handout (p. 135)
- ☐ bowl
- ☐ a bag containing 2 fedora hats, 2 baseball caps, or 2 other "cool" hats; and 2 pairs of "cool" sunglasses
- ☐ copies of "Thank-You Pop-Up" handout (p. 139)
- ☐ scissors
- ☐ glue sticks

LESSON AIM

To help kids realize that ★ *God wants us to serve others.*

OBJECTIVES

Kids will

- ✓ play "Cast of the Castle" to try to improve their position in the castle,
- ✓ participate in an interactive Bible passage about James' and John's request of Jesus,
- ✓ create thank-you cards to give to servantlike people in their lives, and
- ✓ commit to finding ways to be servants of God this week.

BIBLE BASIS

 Mark 10:35–45

"Teacher," said James and John, the sons of Zebedee, "we want you to do us a favor."

Jesus answered with a question: "What is your request?"

"When you sit on your glorious throne, we want to sit in places of honor next to you, one on your right and the other on your left," they replied.

I don't know about you, but I'd shrink at the thought of making such a request. I'd have liked it if James and John had immediately realized how foolish they sounded, blushed, and run to hide behind the nearest rock.

But these two, whom Jesus nicknamed the Sons of Thunder (Mark 3:17), were quite sincere and shockingly bold in their request. And not without some reason. First, they were part of Jesus' "inner three" who were invited to witness things the rest of the disciples weren't. Second, they were probably related to Jesus through their mother, Salome. Many scholars assume that Salome was a sister of Mary, making James and John cousins of Jesus. At the very least Salome was one of the inner circle of women who followed and supported Jesus. She stayed with Jesus at the foot of the cross and was one of the women who went to minister to Jesus' body and found the tomb empty.

It's customary for relatives of those in power to obtain favors based on family connections even today. So perhaps the sons of Zebedee weren't quite as out of line as they appear to be at first. Still, the fault lay in so completely misunderstanding what sort of kingdom Jesus intended to establish. The two hoped that Jesus' popularity would result in a political coup, knocking the long-despised Herods out of power and eventually sending the hated Romans out of the land.

And we wonder how was it that the disciples who'd spent so much time with Jesus still held out hopes for an *earthly* kingdom. In hindsight, it's easy for us to see how mistaken they were, but for those who'd witnessed miracle after miracle, the thought of Jesus submitting to apparent defeat was the furthest thing from their minds. So at this point in Jesus' journey, the sons of Zebedee demonstrated enough chutzpah to upset the other 10 disciples and to show Jesus that they still had no idea about what the kingdom of heaven would be like. They hoped to share in earthly power and glory beside a ruler such as history had never seen.

Jesus must have looked at these two special friends with a loving mixture of sadness and amusement. He challenged them, "Are you able to drink from the bitter cup of suffering I am about to drink?" Jesus knew that later they would freely give their lives for the kingdom of God: James would be one of the first disciples to be martyred, and Acts shows John boldly preaching the gospel at great personal risk. Time would ultimately show all the disciples that ★ *God wants us to serve others.* "Among you it will be different. Whoever wants to be a leader among you must be your servant, and whoever wants to be first among you must be the slave of everyone else."

All Together Now

📖 **Isaiah 52:13–15**

The message of the suffering servant in Isaiah wasn't completely new to the people of Israel. It's just that they wanted a *liberating* messiah so much more. And the promise of someone who'd sit on David's throne made them think of David the conquering king who brought political peace and stability to Israel—not the psalm-writer David who was a man after God's own heart.

Jesus definitely had the crowd magnetism a leader would need. A miracle or two and he could easily have had all Jerusalem at his feet. And just weeks before his death, that earthly power potential was all that even his closest disciples could see.

But the way of Jesus is a different path. It's the way of the cross. As Paul said in Philippians 1:21, "For to me, living means living for Christ, and dying is even better." That's not a popular way to look at things in our society. It takes some spiritual depth to embrace this path. But this concept has always been a part of God's will.

When we choose the path of the suffering servant, we never walk it alone. We never worry about outcomes. Life's glories and failings are as one to us. For we live to do one thing and one thing only: to reflect the pure love of the One we follow.

UNDERSTANDING YOUR KIDS

We live in a competitive society that glorifies "winners." It starts with baby genius programs guaranteed to make a child the smartest in the class and goes on to national spelling bees, sports championships, Olympics, scholarship competitions, and on and on.

I raised one child who busted the top out of everything. My next child, two years younger, had a severe learning disability. I'm glad child two came along. He taught me everything I know about teaching, about what's truly important, and about what we all need to be valuing in kids.

In this lesson you'll be introducing your kids to some of Jesus' "upside-down" teaching about what it means to be first and last. Use it to help kids challenge the way society crowns a few and ignores most.

Prep Box

Beforehand, copy the "Cast of the Castle" handout, cut out the roles, and drop them into a bowl. Make sure you have enough roles for your typical number of kids, and add a few extras in case you have guests.

ATTENTION GRABBER

King of the Castle

Say: **Today we're going to start out in a castle. It may look like our regular room to you, but for right now it's our castle. As you know, a castle is full of people, great and small, so I have a part for everyone to play. To begin, please draw the part you'll play out of this bowl.**

Have kids draw parts. It's OK if not all roles are taken, but make sure that you have at least one child who's royalty and several who are servants. Then form a circle on the floor and let kids read their parts aloud.

Afterward, ask:

• **Tell who has the best part and why.**

Name one of the "lowly" parts, such as the cook or the mouse in the kitchen. Tell kids with this part that they can exchange roles with anyone they choose. All they have to do is stand up and exchange parts. Kids who are chosen must change roles. If no one wants to change roles, draw again and tell kids that they must change roles this time.

Next, tell the person who had his or her part switched that having a part switched isn't a very good deal, and he or she can stand and exchange parts with anyone.

Keep going, with the last person having a part taken away exchanging parts with another person. Then have kids put all the parts back in the bowl.

Say: **We're going to play again, but this time keep your part secret—don't tell anyone. When I invite you to switch parts with someone, you can choose to take me up on my offer or pass and keep the part you have. You don't know what you might get; you only know what part you have. Don't say anything about your part out loud. At the end you'll have a chance to tell what part you started with and what part you ended up with.**

In this round, offer a chance to change parts to the child on your left. Proceed around the circle to the left. To make it extra fun, join in this round yourself.

When you've been around the circle once, ask kids whether they want to stop or go around the circle again. Responses may be about half and half, so decide whether you have time to go around the circle again. If you do, go to the right this time.

Say: **Now we're all curious about the parts everyone**

Cast of the Castle

King or Queen	**King or Queen**	**Prince or Princess**
Prince or Princess	**Cook**	**Mouse in the kitchen**
Servant	**Servant**	**Servant**
Servant	**Servant**	**Servant**
Servant	**Servant**	**Servant**

Published in *All Together Now, Volume 2* by Group Publishing, Inc., 1515 Cascade Ave., Loveland, CO 80538.

135

started with and finished with. I'll begin. I started as a
_____ and ended as a _____. Now let's hear about the rest
of you!

Proceed around the circle to the left until everyone has shared.

Say: **Everyone who ended up a servant, please stand up.
I'd like to shake your hands, because you're the real winners
in this game. That's right! Because in our Bible passage,
Jesus says that ★ *God wants us to serve others.* He says that
if you want to be great, you need to be a *servant*. How about
that!**

**It's kind of crazy that even though Jesus taught that and
acted as a servant to people, it's hard to understand.**

Ask:

• **Tell about someone here at church who is a servant.**

Remind kids to include people who set up and clean up.

Say: **Jesus says that these servants are the greatest of all.
Isn't that amazing?**

**This whole discussion started because of what two
disciples asked Jesus to give them. Let's find out what they
asked for—and about the big argument that followed.**

BIBLE EXPLORATION
....

Who's the Greatest? (Mark 10:35-45)

Say: **Jesus called many disciples, but there were 12 he
called to be especially close to him. In time, these 12 would
be known as the apostles.**

**Jesus had three special friends he took with him on
important occasions. Those three special friends were Peter,
James, and John. Two of those men, James and John, were
probably Jesus' cousins. Peter had a close relationship with
Jesus, but he wasn't family like James and John.**

**All this made James and John think Jesus should treat
them differently from everyone else.**

Pull two fedoras (or the two other "cool" hats) and two pairs of
"cool" sunglasses out of a bag. Ask for two willing children to put
them on.

Say: **No doubt about it, James and John thought they were
pretty cool.**

Signal your James and John to show how cool they are.

When the other 10 disciples saw James and John acting

All Together Now

this way, the Bible said it made them "indignant," which is a way of saying they were *angry* or ticked off. They grumbled to each other about it.

Say, "grumble, grumble, grumble" in low tones and encourage the rest of the class to join you.

Say: **Whenever I say "James and John," you two act cool with a double thumbs-up, and the rest of you say, "grumble, grumble, grumble." Let's try that.**

James and John. While James and John act cool, the rest of the kids say, "grumble, grumble, grumble." **Good job. Keep listening for those cues.**

Say: **Here's an amazing fact to think about, too: This big fight happened just before Palm Sunday and Holy Week, at the very end of Jesus' life on earth. The disciples still had it in their heads that Jesus would set himself up as an earthly king, knock the kings like Herod out of Israel, and then beat Rome as well. They still didn't have a clue about what Jesus came to earth to do. Let's all scratch our heads because the disciples didn't have a clue. So when I say *disciples*, all of you scratch your heads.**

Let's try that. Disciples. Pause as kids scratch their heads. Good. Keep listening for that clue, too.

But Jesus wasn't going to make a kingdom and live in a palace. He wanted to rule in people's hearts and teach them to believe in him as their Savior. Jesus was preparing a kingdom that would last forever! But the *disciples* (pause) didn't quite understand that yet.

So one day when they were all walking up to Jerusalem, *James and John* (pause) came to Jesus with a big request.

Signal James and John to come and stand by you and act cool.

Say: **This is probably a bigger request than I'd ever ask of anybody. Listen and see if you'd ever ask for anything like this.**

"Jesus," they said, "we're going to ask a favor of you. And whatever we ask, we want you to do it for us."

Ask:

• **Describe how asking Jesus a favor like that showed him respect or disrespect.**

Say: **But Jesus knew that *James and John* (pause) sometimes asked for special favors. So Jesus didn't scold them. He simply asked them what they wanted.**

***James and John* (pause) answered, "When you sit on your glorious throne, we want to sit in places of honor next to you, on your right and on your left."**

The other *disciples* (pause) kind of had an idea of what was going on, which made them mad, so they grumbled.

Jesus looked at *James and John* (pause) and said, "You don't know what you are asking! Are you able to drink from the bitter cup of suffering I am about to drink?"

James and John (pause) answered eagerly, "Oh, yes! We are able!"

Jesus knew that he was about to suffer and die at the hands of his enemies. But the *disciples* (pause) were still clueless. However, Jesus knew that *James and John* (pause) and the rest of the *disciples* (pause) would one day suffer for believing in Jesus. In fact, *James* (pause) would be the first of the twelve disciples to die for saying that Jesus is Lord. So Jesus said this:

"You will drink from my bitter cup of suffering, but it's not for me to say who will sit by me. God chooses those people."

By now the rest of the *disciples* (pause) were sure that *James and John* (pause) were asking Jesus for some kind of special honor. The *disciples* (pause) put on their angry faces and grumbled louder!

So Jesus turned and talked to all of them. What he had to say was *not* what any of them expected to hear. And it's not what we expect to hear today. So please wrap your hands around your ears, close your eyes, and concentrate as if Jesus were talking straight to you. Here's what he said:

"Whoever wants to be a leader among you must be your servant, and whoever wants to be first among you must be the slave of everyone else. For even the Son of Man came not to be served but to serve others and to give his life as a ransom for many."

Ask:

• What do you think this means?

• When you think of leaders and great people in our world, describe what kinds of people you usually think of.

• How does what Jesus said change what you think about what makes someone great?

I have a fun craft for you that'll help keep you thinking about what Jesus said. Let's get started on that, and see if we can keep thinking about the idea that ★ *God wants us to serve others.*

"Whoever wants to be a leader among you must be your servant...For even the Son of Man came not to be served but to serve others and to give his life as a ransom for many."

MARK 10:43, 45

✿ ✿ ✿

These words of Jesus remind me of

you!

there's something I've got to say to you.

It's...

For all you do!

Thank You!

Published in *All Together Now, Volume 2* by Group Publishing, Inc., 1515 Cascade Ave., Loveland, CO 80538.

139

Thank-You Pop-Ups

Say: **While we're working on these thank-you cards, think about a servantlike person in your life who'd be surprised and happy to receive a card like this from you. This person's someone who lives out how ★ *God wants us to serve others.***

Lead kids through the following steps to complete the pop-up card.

✓ Fold the card in half on the dotted line. Make sure the corners of the card line up. Crease the fold well.

✓ While the card is still folded, trim away the edges of the card on the solid line.

✓ Open the card and fold it in half the long way so the fold runs exactly through the pop-up. Crease the fold well.

✓ While the card is still folded, fold the pop-up section back and forth on the dotted lines. Crease the folds well.

✓ Finally, open the card and fold it in half horizontally again.

✓ As you close the card, pull the pop-up section forward. Each time you open and close the card, the thank-you will pop up!

✓ Rub a glue stick along the top of the card, stopping at the pop-up section and then continuing again after the pop-up section. Rub the top of the card tightly closed.

Say: **Great work on your cards. You've made a surprise note that'll give a smile to the person you chose to receive it.**

Prep Box

Set out copies of the "Thank-You Pop-Up," scissors, and glue sticks. Beforehand, make a completed pop-up card to show kids as a sample.

COMMITMENT

Who, Me? A Servant?

Say: **Form trios with the largest age spread you can—from youngest to oldest.**

Help kids form trios. It's fine to have groups of four if that works best.

Say: **In your groups, please talk about ways you can be servants this week. Before I call time, I'd like each of you to**

All Together Now

have a plan for two ways you're going to be a servant of God this week.

Walk among the groups as they talk, offering ideas as needed.

Give notice two minutes and one minute before the discussion time will be over. Call time and ask a reporter from each group to stand and share some of the ways their group decided to serve.

Say: **Thanks for sharing ideas on how to live out Jesus' idea that** ★ *God wants us to serve others.*

CLOSING

Servants' Prayers

Gather kids for a closing prayer.

Dear Jesus, it can be hard to understand some of the upside-down teaching we heard from you this week. Help us remember it as we deliver our cards and as we follow your example and practice being servants. We love and honor you. In your name, amen.

The Beggar Who Refused to Be Quiet

LESSON AIM

To help kids understand that ★ *we can call Jesus our friend.*

OBJECTIVES

Kids will

✓ encounter a rascally pirate who wants to introduce his biblical ancestor,

✓ enjoy a firsthand encounter with Blind Bartimaeus,

✓ make a "Shout for Jesus!" banner, and

✓ plan specific ways they'll follow Jesus this week.

BIBLE BASIS

 Mark 10:46-52

There was always time for another healing, even when Jesus was nearing the final leg of his journey to Jerusalem, where he would suffer on the cross and die.

Jesus would have been traveling with a group of pilgrims—and excited pilgrims, to be sure—for those lucky enough to have squeezed in close to the unusual young rabbi from Galilee would have enjoyed the pleasure of hearing him teach along the way. This was a typical teaching mode for rabbis, to teach as they walked along. It's not hard to imagine the crowds that wanted to be close to Jesus. Jesus had wreaked some pretty significant mayhem with the Temple leaders each time he'd shown up in Jerusalem. What would happen this year?

You'll need...

☐ makeshift pirate costume (see Attention Grabber)

☐ actor to play Blind Bartimaeus, Bible-times costume

☐ 2 copies of the "Blind Bartimaeus Tells His Story" script (pp. 150-151)

☐ ragged Bible-times costume, ragged blanket, rough walking stick

☐ highlighter

☐ 2 copies per child plus extras of the "Banner Letters" handout (p. 153)

☐ one 40-inch length of burlap ribbon (or other ribbon that appeals to both boys and girls) per child

☐ tacky glue

☐ 1 large wood or glass bead per child

Jewish law stated that all healthy Jewish males over age 12 who lived within 15 miles of Jerusalem must make their Passover in Jerusalem. Those who couldn't make the trip often lined the streets of the main routes toward the Temple city to encourage the pilgrims along their way. So between the crowds around Jesus and those at the city gate and along the road, there was a loud, happy group of people over which one lone, blind beggar was trying to make himself heard. And though he was hushed and shushed by those annoyed by his persistent hollering, Bartimaeus wouldn't give up. For here was his one chance to see Jesus, and he wouldn't be denied.

Go, Bartimaeus!

I think of how many times I've hollered myself hoarse at a football game. But, to be perfectly honest, I'd feel a little silly shouting, "Jesus, son of David, have mercy on me!" And yelling it over and over again, no matter how many people shushed me. I might have given up and cried. But not Bartimaeus. He was going to be heard. And he was! When Jesus finally heard the blind man's cries, he stopped in his tracks.

When Bartimaeus addressed Jesus, he didn't simply call him Rabbi, as our Scripture usually states, but *Rabbouni*, which means "my teacher." Bartimaeus knew the real thing whether he could see Jesus or not. And when Jesus gave Bartimaeus his sight, the man didn't go merrily on his way, but followed Jesus down the road to Jerusalem.

 Psalm 40:1–3, 16

This psalm could be the testimony of Bartimaeus.

Beggars were a common sight in Jesus' time. For disabled folk without family to care for them, begging was their only option. Beggars typically stationed themselves near city gates where, in Roman times, travelers would be reaching into their purses anyway to pay city taxes.

Jewish law required farmers to leave the last gleanings of their fields for the poor, but for the blind and physically disabled, this small benevolence provided little help. Israelites were so heavily taxed during this period that they did well to survive, much less share with those in need. Gaining his sight meant that Bartimaeus could learn a skill and seek employment. But first he answered a higher calling—to follow the man who healed him.

Many saw what Jesus did and were amazed.

All Together Now

How often do particular psalms reflect your life experience? Isn't it splendid that the psalms have voiced the heart cries of so many of us through the ages—even of Jesus himself?

UNDERSTANDING YOUR KIDS

Kids know how to shout—oh yes, they do! Give them any kind of a ball and turn them loose in a room and you'll hear shouting. Put them on a soccer field and you'll hear shouting. Tell a bunch of them that they can have a sleepover and you'll hear shouting. Announce that the sleepover will include an unlimited supply of their favorite pizza and treats and you'll hear more shouting. Put their favorite team in the Super Bowl and you'll hear more shouting. Announce a family trip to Disney World, and you'll have to leave the house temporarily because of the shouting.

But when it comes to Jesus—you won't hear much shouting, unless they're at a great kids' camp. I mean, shouting for Jesus—who does that?

Bartimaeus did, in the face of lots of shushers, and it got him a face-to-face encounter with Jesus and the gift of sight. People at the triumphal entry into Jerusalem shouted, and Jesus said that if they didn't shout his praises, the very rocks would cry out (Luke 19:40).

Use this lesson to teach your kids that ★ *we can call Jesus our friend.*

ATTENTION GRABBER

Pirated Away!

As your kids gather, greet them with a nasty *Aargh!*

Adopt a pirate-y accent and say: **So this is me crew fer the day. Wal, let me 'ave a look at you scurvy lot! Line up, then. An' look mean! I ain't 'avin no one on me crew who don't look mean. 'Ats better. Now lemme 'ear ya say *Aargh!***

Turn to your assistant or an older child and say: **I didn't 'ear nuffin', did you?**

This time, le'mme 'ear ya say *Aargh!*

Pause for the kids to respond.

Say: *Aargh!*

Each time the response gets louder.

Say: *Aargh!*

Look contented after the last response.

Say: **'Ats more like it, me lads 'n' lassies. You wanna be a pirate, you gotta get them *Aarghs* right, else nobody's gonna be skeerd of ya. And I knows wat I'm talkin' about, ya hear? *Aargh!***

Allow time for kids respond.

Say: **Time fer inspection!**

Crack up the kids by lining them up and then checking on them in silly ways, such as opening their mouths and checking their teeth, checking their bones, and having some give you their meanest faces.

Say: **Shiver me timbers! Splash some mud 'n' sea water on ya's and ya might make a pirate crew yet. Kinda disappointin' with not one of ya' havin' a peg leg, though. Anyone got a parrot fer a pet? Me parrot took off fer destinations unknown, and I'm missin' the ole birdie.**

No peg legs and no parrots, eh? Then what're ya 'ere fer, pray tell, if ya ain't got the makin's of a decent crew? Start explainin' that to me right quick, er somebody's gonna walk the plank!

Let kids explain that they're here for Sunday school, not a pirate crew call.

Say: **Sunday school, is it? Oh, eh, now I remember! I came here to introduce my famous ancestor in the Bible.**

Wave your arms and look your meanest.

Say: **What? You don't believe I have a famous ancestor in the Bible? Wal, I surely do or I'm shark bait. Let's see, I** don't think I took time to introduce meself. Let me give ya the pleasure of meetin' me, then. I'm Blind Bart, the most fearsome pirate ye scallywags'll ever meet. That oughta give ya a good enough clue about me famous ancestor, Blind Bart. I'm named after 'im, ya know.

And it was 'im who taught me the importance of sayin' a good *Aargh!*

Aargh!

Pause for the children to respond.

Say: **Ol' Blind Bart could make 'imself 'eard over a 'ole crowd of people, he could. Otherwise, he'd a never met Jesus, an' that be the truth of it!**

Aargh!

Pause for the children to respond.

Say: **I've given ya all the clues I can. Either I send ya all off the plank, or I go and find me crew. Ya scallywags all look too clean 'n' purty ta swab me plank, so I guess I'll leave ya's in peace, as long as ya hurry up an' dig up Ol' Blind Bart's story.**

Head toward the door. Just before you reach the door, stop and say: *Aargh!*

Pause for kids to respond.

Say: *Aargh!*

Pause for kids to respond more loudly.

Say: *Aargh!*

Pause for kids to respond at the top of their voices!

Slip out the door or behind a large obstacle in your room to remove your pirate costume. Then return to your group.

Say: **Hi, kids. Sorry to be a little late this morning. Uh, did anyone else see a pirate ship in our parking lot?**

Let younger kids tell you about the scary pirate who visited.

Ask:

• **What did Blind Bart the pirate tell you to do when he left?**

Say: **Oh, I get it! We're learning today about Blind Bartimaeus. Blind Bartimaeus shouted so loudly that even through a large crowd, Jesus could hear his cries for help.**

Blind Bart the pirate wasn't really Bartimaeus's ancestor, but he certainly gave you an interesting introduction to our story. Maybe something like this?

Aargh!

Pause for kids to respond.

Say: *Aargh!*

Pause for kids to respond more loudly.

Say: **Aargh!**

Pause for kids to respond at the top of their voices!

BIBLE EXPLORATION

The Beggar Who Refused to Be Quiet

(Mark 10:46-52)

Before you begin the story, have kids spread out around your room and stand up.

Say: **Today, you're going to help me tell about what really happened to Blind Bartimeaus. Let me set the background for today's Bible story. There are no pirates involved, I promise. But when I tell you what the people did, your job is to act it out. I'll give you cues to follow. Ready? Here we go.**

Jesus and lots of other people were traveling up to Jerusalem for the Passover feast. Sling your heavy bag over your shoulder and walk in place. Demonstrate how heavy your pretend bag is and wipe your brow as you walk in place. **This was an exciting time in the Jewish year. The law said that every Jewish male over age 12 who lived near Jerusalem** *had* **to travel to Jerusalem for Passover. And Jews from all over Israel made the trip to Jerusalem. Keep walking! Boy, these bags are heavy!**

People traveled in family groups and in groups from towns and districts. Help kids find two or three partners to walk alongside. **Everyone sang special songs as they traveled, children played, and they all camped at night, made cheerful campfires, cooked what they'd brought along for food, and shared stories. Stop walking for the night, and choose whether you'll sing, jump rope, or make a campfire and cook.** Demonstrate pretending to sing, jumping rope, and making a campfire and cooking, and lead kids through all three motions for about 30 seconds.

Everyone freeze in place! One thing the Israelites ate was flat bread baked over hot rocks and salted fish. Maybe that doesn't sound quite as good as what we have today, but let's eat anyway. Have kids pretend to eat and make yucky faces.

OK, time to walk again. Put your bag back over your shoulder and walk. As they passed through towns, people

Prep Box

Beforehand, choose an adult or young adult male to play Blind Bartimaeus as kids act out the story. Give this person a copy of the "Blind Bartimaeus Tells His Story" script a week before so he can become familiar with the story. Make a ragged Bible-times costume available to him. Encourage him to wear old leather sandals or to come barefoot, and to rub dirt or charcoal on his arms, face and legs, since a roadside beggar would not have been clean! He can also carry a ragged blanket and rough walking stick. Encourage this person to essentially memorize the script so he won't have to read while portraying blind Bartimaeus.

Prepare a second script for a child you'll recruit to play Jesus in the middle of the story. Clearly highlight Jesus' lines in this copy of the script.

All Together Now

who couldn't make the pilgrimage stood beside the road to wave and cheer travelers and family members along. It was like one giant festival for the entire country. Let's pretend to be the crowd, waving and cheering on the travelers. Wave and cheer with kids, saying things such as, "Be safe!" "Have a nice journey!" and "Don't get blisters!"

Back then, if you got to travel close to a famous rabbi like Jesus, you were especially lucky, because rabbis taught as they walked along. People who'd never heard Jesus before probably wanted to get close to him so they could see why everyone was excited about him. Bring forward the child who you've chosen to play Jesus, and encourage the rest of the kids to move closer to this child as they continue to walk.

Of course this was a great opportunity for the poor beggars, too. The travelers were in a good mood (cue everyone to smile big), so they gave what alms, or money, they could to beggars who were lucky enough to get close to the road where travelers would pass by. Demonstrate flipping coins out to pretend beggars. A city gate was one of the best places for a beggar, because travelers had to stop and pay taxes when entering a city.

This is the cue for Blind Bartimaeus to bang loudly on your door.

Say: **I wonder who that could be.**

Have a child answer the door. Blind Bartimaeus enters and continues the story, while you continue giving cues for kids to respond.

Blind Bartimaeus Tells His Story

BARTIMAEUS: Alms for the poor! Alms for the poor! Oh, uh, hello. Can you help me find the side of the road?

Encourage children to help Bartimaeus.

BARTIMAEUS: God bless you for your kindness to a poor beggar. I've heard that Jesus will be here soon and I want to meet him.

Encourage the crowd of kids to move around the child playing Jesus so he or she is obscured.

BARTIMAEUS: I know I'm just a beggar, but I'm determined to meet Jesus. I've heard he's healed many blind people. This is my chance to meet him!** *(Bartimaeus wanders around, feeling for obstacles and bumping into the crowd.)*

Tell children to help you move Bartimaeus away from the main traffic so he's not crushed by the crowd.

BARTIMAEUS: Stop moving me! How am I going to meet Jesus if I'm way back here? I must meet Jesus! He can heal me! I'm going to meet Jesus no matter what it takes.** *(Bartimaeus pushes back into the crowd of kids.)*

Move Jesus through the crowd of kids toward Bartimaeus, and encourage kids to chant: **Jesus is coming! Jesus is coming! Jesus is coming! Jesus is coming! Jesus is coming!**

BARTIMAEUS: *(simultaneously as kids chant and loudly)* **Jesus, Son of David! Have mercy on me!**

All Together Now

Move Jesus close to Bartimaeus and encourage kids to continue chanting loudly: **Hurray for Jesus! Hurray for Jesus! Hurray for Jesus! Hurray for Jesus!**

BARTIMAEUS: *(simultaneously and even more loudly)* **Jesus, Son of David! Have mercy on me!**

TEACHER: *(to Bartimaeus)* **Why don't you stop being such a nuisance?! Hush!**

BARTIMAEUS: Jesus, Son of David! Have mercy on me!

Move Jesus to right in front of Bartimaeus.

BARTIMAEUS: Jesus, Son of David! Have mercy on me!

Stop kids from chanting and point out that Jesus has come face to face with Bartimaeus. Have kids change their chant to: **Jesus wants to see you!**

Signal silence for the entire group, and then have the child playing Jesus say: **What do you want?**

BARTIMAEUS: *(reaches out for Jesus)* **Beloved rabbi, I want to see!**

Encourage Jesus to say kindly: **Your faith has made you well. Now go your way.**

BARTIMAEUS: *(in shock)* **I can see! I can see!** *(Turns and looks all around.)* **I can see!**

Tell everyone to get back into a crowd to follow Jesus as he walks down the road and begins the journey again.

BARTIMAEUS: I'm going to follow Jesus! *(Runs to catch up with Jesus.)*

Permission to photocopy this handout granted for local church use. Copyright © Lois Keffer. Published in *All Together Now, Volume 2* by Group Publishing, Inc., 1515 Cascade Ave., Loveland, CO 80538.

Say: **How about a round of applause for everyone? Thank you for bringing this story to life!**

LIFE APPLICATION

Shout for Jesus! Banners

Lead kids through the following steps to complete their banners. Have older children help the younger ones with this craft.

- ✓ Line up the two handouts, one exactly on top of the other, and cut out all the letter rectangles.
- ✓ Place the letters so they spell, "Shout for Jesus!" vertically, with one letter facing up and one letter facing down, so the finished banner will be two-sided.
- ✓ Knot the top of the ribbon, and then glue the letters in order to the front and back of the ribbon, leaving extra space between words.
- ✓ Slide a bead onto the ribbon bottom of the banner to add weight; then tie a knot to hold the bead in place.
- ✓ Let the banners lie flat for the remainder of class to let the tacky glue dry.

As kids finish, encourage them to tell you where they will display their "Shout for Jesus!" banners in their homes.

Say: ★ *We can call Jesus our friend.* **Bartimaeus didn't have any problem shouting out for Jesus even when others told him to hush. He wanted to call Jesus his friend.**

Think hard about this.

Ask:

• **Tell what it means to you to call Jesus your friend.**

• **Why do you think Bartimaeus, a blind beggar who had never met Jesus before, wasn't afraid to call out for Jesus?**

• **How can you remember to call out for your friend Jesus when you need him?**

Say: **Use your banner to help remind you that** ★ *we can call Jesus our friend.*

Prep Box

At your craft table, set out scissors, 40-inch lengths of burlap ribbon, tacky glue, and copies of the "Banner Letters" handout. You'll need two copies of the handout for each child. Have a finished "Shout for Jesus!" banner on hand for kids to see.

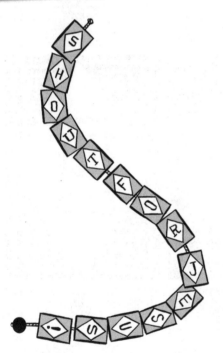

Banner Letters

Published in *All Together Now, Volume 2* by Group Publishing, Inc., 1515 Cascade Ave., Loveland, CO 80538.

COMMITMENT

Jesus' Instant Follower

Say: **There's another surprising thing that Bartimaeus did besides shouting for Jesus. He left his begging spot and followed Jesus right away.**

That's surprising. Someone else might have been a little curious about what the world looked like or what the people who helped him might have looked like.

Ask:

• **What do you think about Bartimaeus' decision to leave a place that was familiar to him and follow Jesus?**

• **What kinds of things keep us from following Jesus the way Bartimaeus did?**

• **What would it take for you to drop everything and follow Jesus like that?**

Say: **Get into groups of three and brainstorm ways you can follow Jesus this week. Decide on at least two ways you'll follow Jesus like you've never followed him before. Be ready in two minutes for one person in your group to report on ways people in your trio have decided to follow Jesus this week.**

When time is up, let each group tell about what they'll do.

CLOSING

Closing Prayer

Gather kids for a closing prayer. Explain that you'll pray part of the prayer, and then kids will finish the prayer by telling ways they'll call Jesus their friend this week.

Pray: **Dear Jesus, today we've learned that ★ *we can call you our friend*. Help us remember to call out for you when...** (pause for children to add times when they'll remember to call on Jesus). **Help us get better and better at calling you our friend, Lord. In your name, amen.**

All Together Now

It's your holiday
swiss army knife!

Seasonal Specials for Children's Ministry:

All-New Ideas for 13 Holidays

Tired of tired holiday ideas? Need "icing" for your Sunday morning? This book is chock-full of fun and practical ideas for all the major holidays, including Easter, Independence Day, Thanksgiving, Christmas, and more. Best of all, every idea interactively connects kids to Jesus through the year's celebrations we enjoy together.

Covering preschool—6th grade, *Seasonal Specials* handles 13 holidays, each one with step-by-step instructions for:

- crafts
- snacks
- devotions
- games
- songs
- skits
- service projects
- plus "Extra Specials" including tips, jokes, factoids, and fingerplays

You'll love *Seasonal Specials* because:

- you'll get fun, new, timely holiday ideas to make or add to your own lessons
- kids can make a Christian connection to their favorite holidays
- you can address holidays from a biblical perspective

▶ ISBN 978-0-7644-7991-5 • $24.99 *In Canada $27.49*

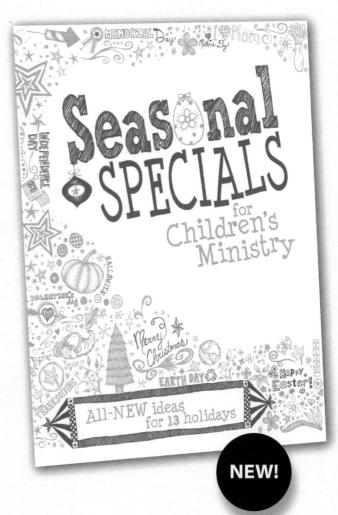

NEW!

Secret weapons for *getting kids' attention!*